WORLD HISTORY

THE SCIENTIFIC REVOLUTION

HOW SCIENCE AND TECHNOLOGY SHAPED THE WORLD

By Caroline Kennon

Portions of this book originally appeared in *The Scientific Revolution* by Don Nardo.

LUCENT
PRESS

Published in 2019 by
Lucent Press, an Imprint of Greenhaven Publishing, LLC
353 3rd Avenue
Suite 255
New York, NY 10010

Designer: Deanna Paternostro
Editor: Siyavush Saidan

Cataloging-in-Publication Data

Names: Kennon, Caroline.
Title: The scientific revolution: how science and technology shaped the world / Caroline Kennon.
Description: New York : Lucent Press, 2019. | Series: World history | Includes index.
Identifiers: ISBN 9781534563902 (pbk.) | ISBN 9781534563889 (library bound) | ISBN 9781534563896
(ebook)
Subjects: LCSH: Discoveries in science–History–Juvenile literature. | Science–History–Juvenile literature.
Classification: LCC Q180.55.D57 K46 2019 | DDC 509–dc23

Printed in the United States of America

CPSIA compliance information: Batch #BS18KL: For further information contact Greenhaven Publishing LLC, New York, New York at 1-844-317-7404.

Please visit our website, www.greenhavenpublishing.com. For a free color catalog of all our
high-quality books, call toll free 1-844-317-7404 or fax 1-844-317-7405.

Contents

Foreword

History books are often filled with names and dates—words and numbers for students to memorize for a test and forget once they move on to another class. However, what history books should be filled with are great stories, because the history of our world is filled with great stories. Love, death, violence, heroism, and betrayal are not just themes found in novels and movie scripts. They are often the driving forces behind major historical events.

When told in a compelling way, fact is often far more interesting—and sometimes far more unbelievable—than fiction. World history is filled with more drama than the best television shows, and all of it really happened. As readers discover the incredible truth behind the triumphs and tragedies that have impacted the world since ancient times, they also come to understand that everything is connected. Historical events do not exist in a vacuum. The stories that shaped world history continue to shape the present and will undoubtedly shape the future.

The titles in this series aim to provide readers with a comprehensive understanding of pivotal events in world history. They are written with a focus on providing readers with multiple perspectives to help them develop an appreciation for the complexity of the study of history. There is no set lens through which history must be viewed, and these titles encourage readers to analyze different viewpoints to understand why a historical figure acted the way they did or why a contemporary scholar wrote what they did about a historical event. In this way, readers are able to sharpen their critical-thinking skills and apply those skills in their history classes. Readers are aided in this pursuit by formally documented quotations and annotated bibliographies, which encourage further research and debate.

Many of these quotations come from carefully selected primary sources, including diaries, public records, and contemporary research and writings. These valuable primary sources help readers hear the voices of those who directly experienced historical events, as well as the voices of biographers and historians who provide a unique perspective on familiar topics. Their voices all help history come alive in a vibrant way.

As students read the titles in this series, they are provided with clear context in the form of maps, timelines, and informative text. These elements give them the basic facts they need to fully appreciate the high drama that is history.

The study of history is difficult at times—not because of all the information that needs to be memorized but because of the challenging questions it asks us. How could something as horrible as the Holocaust happen? Why would religious leaders use torture during the Inquisition? Why does ISIS have so many followers? The information presented in each title gives readers the tools they need to confront these questions and participate in the debates they inspire.

As we pore over the stories of events and eras that changed the world, we come to understand a simple truth: No one can escape being a part of history. We are not bystanders; we are active participants in the stories that are being created now and will be written about in history books decades and even centuries from now. The titles in this series help readers gain a deeper appreciation for history and a stronger understanding of the connection between the stories of the past and the stories they are part of right now.

SETTING THE SCENE: A TIMELINE

1543   **1597**   **1609–1633**

Nicolaus Copernicus publishes *On the Revolutions of the Heavenly Spheres,* claiming the sun is the center of the universe and marking the beginning of the Scientific Revolution; Andreas Vesalius publishes *On the Fabric of the Human Body,* in which he urges medical researchers to conduct their own human dissections.

Galileo builds his version of a telescope and sees for his own eyes that Earth is not the center of the universe; the Catholic Church bans *On the Revolutions of the Heavenly Spheres* on the basis of heresy; Galileo is forced by the Catholic Church to renounce his belief in a sun-centered universe.

Galileo Galilei admits privately to Johannes Kepler that he believes Copernicus was right about a sun-centered universe.

Isaac Newton publishes
*Mathematical Principles
of Natural Philosophy*,
which includes his famous
three laws of motion.

The Royal Society is
established and determines
that experimental evidence is
always superior to theoretical
evidence; Antonie van
Leeuwenhoek uses his
microscopes to discover
tiny creatures swimming in
all materials, such as liquids,
food, and human waste.

The term "Scientific Revolution"
is popularized by historian
Alexandre Koyré.

A NEW SCIENCE

Science is a subject that is taught in school to familiarize students with how the universe works. Students learn a large scope of complicated concepts—from how the planets revolve around the sun to how human beings unconsciously pump oxygen in and out of their lungs. Every year, science makes important advances as those who study it learn more and more about the natural world. Modern science, which most students learn about, has its roots in a period call the Scientific Revolution. This era witnessed a series of scientific events and discoveries, occurring mostly in Europe in early modern times. The Scientific Revolution consisted of developments in math, chemistry, biology, physics, and astronomy, which changed the way the world thought and learned. These developments happened over a span of two centuries—from about the mid-1500s to the mid-1700s.

Most historians recognize the publication of Polish astronomer Nicolaus Copernicus's *On the Revolutions of the Heavenly Spheres* in 1543 as the official beginning of the Scientific Revolution. The book claimed the radical idea that Earth—and the other planets—revolve around the sun. Before that, the assumption was that all the heavenly bodies (which is a term used to describe planets, moons, and stars) revolved around a stationary Earth. In contrast, no specific event marked the conclusion of the Scientific Revolution. The great English scientist Isaac Newton died in 1727, and most modern experts feel that in the two or three generations that followed, the Scientific Revolution blended into the enormous flood of new scientific discoveries that were made in Europe and elsewhere. The mid-1700s marked a turning point in history where, for the first time, huge portions of

Europeans started to believe in the power of science to prove things that were previously unquestioned—such as the rotation of Earth around the sun.

It is important to emphasize, however, that both the concept and dating of the Scientific Revolution are products of modern science. Copernicus, Newton, and their fellow thinkers had no notion that they were in the midst of a specific scientific era. In fact, the term "Scientific Revolution" was not coined until 1939 (by historian Alexandre Koyré), and its first use in a book title was not until 1954. The term was part of an effort by modern historians to better understand scientific trends in past ages.

Science Revolts Against Religion

More important to modern scholars than when exactly the Scientific Revolution took place is why it happened when it did. One reason they often cite is that in the 1500s and 1600s, the Roman Catholic Church was beginning to lose its iron grip on European minds. For centuries, the church had been Europe's most powerful and influential institution. In medieval times, the pope and other church leaders, based in Rome, Italy, were the moderators of European social standards, including education. The church controlled what was taught in schools, and those ideas were rooted mainly in the Bible. Priests, bishops,

and other interpreters of that holy book strongly believed that the sun moved around Earth, which lay at the center of the universe.

Over time, Europe's kings grew more powerful and began to challenge the church's authority. In the early 1500s, the Protestant Reformation challenged and shook the Catholic Church's foundations. As a result, the authority of the pope and bishops started to decrease, especially among those thinkers who were on the cutting edge of science. In prior decades, such men were arrested or burned at the stake for communicating ideas that contradicted biblical tradition, but eventually, the church was unable to stop the onrushing tide of new scientific concepts. The danger of science to the church was that it might contradict the Bible and possibly become the new highest authority.

With science emerging in direct opposition to religion, non-religious learning centers were being established for the sake of scientific inquiry. Scholars and students were attracted to these growing scientific centers across the European continent, and newly established universities started teaching a wide range of scientific subjects. The royal courts in England, Belgium, the Netherlands, western Germany, and parts of Italy offered money and other support for naturalists—thinkers interested in exploring and explaining nature. The invention of the printing press in the 15th century provided a much more efficient means of distributing new scientific ideas throughout Europe in only weeks or months. In prior ages, such ideas had taken years or even decades to become known to a majority of the population. With printed books and a growing enthusiasm for knowledge, new generations of young Europeans were inspired to study scientific concepts.

Science at Sea

Perhaps the biggest and most influential cause for the rise of modern science from the 1500s to the 1700s was the rapid expansion of the known world and the economic, social, and other changes it brought. Beginning in the late 1400s, European explorers sailed around the African continent and to North and South America. In addition, in 1522, the vessels originally launched by Spain's Ferdinand Magellan returned from the first ever journey around the world. These explorations across the globe opened up vast new trade routes, which allowed European kings, nobles, merchants, and bankers to grow rich. The voyages also stimulated the production of new inventions to make sailing and navigation more efficient and profitable. Many of these inventions involved using the stars as navigational tools, which resulted in many scientists becoming interested in astronomy. Multiple

scientists aided advancement in this particular field; Isaac Newton's lunar theory along with Edmond Halley's lunar tables, which studied the moon's movements, were among the most important advancements of their time.

While astronomers and mathematicians wrestled with finding better means of navigation, other researchers tried to find new and better industrial methods of production and more effective tools and weapons. Still others expanded into the medical sciences in order to help sailors stay healthy on long voyages. At the same time, geographers rushed to create more accurate maps, and inventors and machinists built more effective clocks and watches. In addition, huge amounts of new knowledge about other parts of the world poured into Europe. The discovery of new plant and animal species, as well as entirely new civilizations of fellow humans, inspired numerous scientific discussions and theories among Europe's educated classes.

Unstoppable Progress

The various events leading into the Scientific Revolution meant that once modern science was in full swing, it could not be stopped—or even slowed. In time, it produced a more technically oriented—and in many ways, more convenient—world. Modern science continues to emphasize the idea that, given the time and

Ferdinand Magellan's voyage around the world was a huge advancement in sea exploration.

the means, human beings can and will unravel the mysteries of nature and use that knowledge to create a better world. In the words of scholar Lisa Jardine,

> The pursuit of science in the seventeenth century was an engaged, imaginative and even adventurous affair. It brought together creative talents of all kinds, from all walks of life ... science galvanized [stimulated] an entire continent, driving knowledge forward at an astonishing speed. It broke down international barriers [and] broadened the horizons not just of the small circle of active [scientists] but of entire communities. It heralded those everyday technologies that have allowed all of us, women and men alike, more or better opportunities to expand our individual understandings [of the world], increase our experience and, above all, learn.[1]

CHAPTER ONE

GRANDFATHERS OF SCIENCE

The roots of Western civilization's collective scientific knowledge overwhelmingly come from the ancient Greeks. Even when Nicolaus Copernicus proposed that the universe might be sun-centered in 1543, it was difficult for Europeans to adjust and change their worldview. The Greeks were considered the authorities on the universe, with intelligence that far surpassed anyone who came later. Aristotle and Claudius Ptolemy had strong reputations as philosopher-scientists, and they claimed that Earth was the center of all existence. However, these men failed to actually conduct any experiments. In fact, many prestigious Greeks were deliberately opposed to an experimental method for testing knowledge.

Generation after generation of Greeks and Romans blindly accepted Aristotle's views, sometimes using them as a basis upon which to build new theories. Ptolemy constructed a sky map of the positions of 1,022 stars within 48 constellations—a map that would be used for the next 15 centuries. Aristotle and Ptolemy were very wrong about the workings of the solar system, but there were other theories that turned out to be true. It became the responsibility of the Scientific Revolution to recognize which theories were mistakes and to correct them.

The *Physis*

The Greek invention of science began about 600 BC. For countless centuries before that time, people everywhere, including Greece, thought that the universe, natural occurrences, and human destiny were all the products of the whims of various gods or other supernatural forces. The first Greek thinkers, who are now seen as the earliest scientists, rejected that concept. They viewed the universe as a

Copernicus kicked off the Scientific Revolution by claiming that the universe was sun-centered (heliocentric), not Earth-centered (geocentric).

ARISTARCHUS OF SAMOS

Nearly 2,000 years before Copernicus described a heliocentric model of the solar system, Aristarchus of Samos made the first claim. Aristarchus was an ancient Greek astronomer and mathematician, born in 310 BC. He identified the sun as the central, glowing point of the universe, with all the planets rotating around it. He used geometry to determine (incorrectly) that the sun is about 20 times further away from Earth than the moon is. The sun is actually 400 times further away from Earth than the moon. Aristarchus's mistake came from determining that the angle between the sun and the moon was 87 degrees, when it actually is about 89 degrees. His only surviving work is titled *On the Sizes and Distances of the Sun and Moon*.

rational, ordered place that worked according to underlying scientific principles. Furthermore, they argued, humans possess the mental ability to discover and explain those principles. As many Greek scientists were also philosophers, they relied heavily on logic and rational observation to make their scientific claims. This marked the first time in history that humans turned inward, instead of outward toward the gods, to explain the world.

Employing this new, rational approach to understanding nature, the first few generations of Greek scientists observed and discussed many diverse aspects of nature. Their efforts laid the groundwork for most of the major scientific disciplines, including astronomy, physics, chemistry, biology, mechanics, and medicine. At first, these disciplines were not viewed as separate subjects, as science itself was not yet seen as separate from philosophy. These early thinkers are often referred to as philosopher-scientists.

The first philosopher-scientist to have a major impact on later scientific thought was Thales of Miletus (a large Greek city on the western coast of Anatolia, or modern-day Turkey). Like other early Greek thinkers, he searched for what they called the *physis*, from which the modern words "physical" and "physics" are taken. The Greeks defined it as nature's main underlying physical principle. After much contemplation, Thales decided that the *physis* was water. Aristotle later wrote, "He got the notion probably

Thales of Miletus searched for the foundation of nature; he concluded that it was water.

Greek thinker Empedocles believed that before humans existed, many different species had lived on Earth but died off because they could not adapt.

from seeing that the nutriment of all things is moist, and that heat itself is generated by the moist and kept alive by it ... and that the [basis] of all creatures has a moist nature, and water is the origin of the nature of moist things."[2]

Other early Greek thinkers, including some of Thales's own students, suggested different substances for the *physis*. One of these students, Anaximander, believed that nature's principal underlying material was an everlasting, invisible substance he called the "Boundless." This substance, he claimed, somehow gave rise to the four classical elements that the Greek thinkers believed made up everything in the cosmos: earth, water, air, and fire. Anaximander also tackled the mystery of the origins of life. He proposed that the first living creatures existed in the sea and that, over time, some of them crawled onto the dry land and adapted themselves to their new environment. He also claimed that humans came into being in a similar manner. A later Greek thinker named Empedocles developed these concepts further. Before humans arrived, he speculated, numerous and diverse species had existed. Some of them were not well adapted to survive in the harsh conditions they lived in, so they became extinct, and stronger, more flexible species took

their place. A later ancient writer summed up Empedocles's theory this way:

These and other such monstrous and misshapen births were created. But all in vain. Nature [prevented] them from [continuing]. They could not gain the coveted flower of maturity nor procure food nor [produce offspring]. For it is evident that many contributory factors are essential to be able to forge the chain of a species ... Every species that you now see drawing the breath of life has been protected and preserved ... either by cunning or by courage or by speed.[3]

Empedocles did not follow up on this evolutionary theory or attempt to collect a wide array of evidence to support it. Neither did any other Greek scientist. More than 2,000 years later, an English researcher named Charles Darwin gathered the necessary evidence to support this same principle, which he called natural selection. The fact that Empedocles expressed an early form of the truth so many centuries ago demonstrates that the ancient Greeks were every bit as smart as people are today. However, their lack of experiments and resources kept them from properly developing many of their ideas.

$A^2 + B^2 = C^2$

Pythagoras of Samos was a Greek philosopher and mathematician, and he is well known today for the Pythagorean theorem, which states that on a right triangle, the square of the side of the triangle opposite the right angle is equal to the sum of the squares of the other two sides. This formula is taught in schools all over the world. Pythagoras and his followers suggested that the *physis* was made up of numbers, not material elements. He believed that all objects in nature were shaped by mathematical relationships and these relationships were balanced with one another. Pythagoras's ideas greatly influenced Plato and all of Western philosophy.

Pythagoras believed that all objects in nature were shaped by math.

Everyone Has a Theory

Greek scientists continued to produce many ingenious theories in order to explain how nature works. Some of these theories were correct, but others were not. One of Empedocles's contemporaries, Anaxagoras, also advanced a theory to explain the origins of living things based on his own explanation of the *physis*. Anaxagoras put forward the concept that tiny "seeds" of all the tangible substances known to humanity exist deep inside all things. This idea was based partly on his observations of the act and consequences of eating. He pointed out that when people eat bread, fruits, and vegetables, they grow flesh, bones, skin, and hair. This could not occur, he said, unless the "seeds" of flesh, bones, skin, and hair were present in the food when it was eaten. How else, he asked, could hair come from something that was not hair in the first place? Thus, Anaxagoras proposed, everything contained tiny pieces of everything else.

Many Greeks rejected an early form of the atomic theory. Leucippus and Democritus, both of whom lived in the 400s BC, proposed that all matter is made up of tiny, invisible particles called atoms. The word "atom" in ancient Greek means "indivisible." However, Aristotle, who became the most influential of the Greek philosopher-scientists, rejected the concept of atoms, so it never came into wide favor in ancient times. Fortunately, it survived, mainly in the writings of the Greek thinker Epicurus and the Roman philosopher Lucretius. Centuries later, in the early 1800s, atomic theory made a comeback when scientists discovered that matter was made up of atoms after all.

Studying the Greeks

When the Western Roman Empire fell in the fifth and sixth centuries, Latin became the official language of both the Catholic Church and scholarship. Latin manuscripts were preserved in Europe, while most Greek works in science and other subjects were set aside and forgotten. That included many of Aristotle's writings. All was not completely lost, however. From the early 600s to roughly 1100, a flourishing Islamic culture burst from the Arabian Peninsula and spread across the Middle East, North Africa, and southern Spain. Muslim leaders encouraged learning and scientific inquiry. Educated Muslims eagerly read the ancient Greek scientific works, which had remained in circulation in parts of the Middle East, and translated many of them into Arabic. When the Muslims and Christians came into contact during the Crusades, these Arabic versions of the Greek manuscripts slowly but steadily filtered into Europe. There, they were translated once again, this time into Latin.

In this way, Aristotle, Ptolemy, and other Greek scientists came to be read and studied in Europe in late medieval times. Not only did these long-dead Greeks appear to be wise sages of a great and powerful past civilization, their strongly geocentric views of the universe perfectly matched those of the Catholic Church. Aristotle's astronomical theories harmonized with many concepts promoted by the Catholic Church. As a result, he became the

Aristotle was respected as one of the ultimate scientific authorities for centuries.

accepted authority on science, math, and philosophy, largely unquestioned for hundreds of years.

A Call for Proof

By the early 1400s, in the midst of the European Renaissance, several ancient Greek scientists, especially Aristotle, were considered reliable sources of knowledge. The church enthusiastically endorsed these revered figures, and its hold over European society was stronger than it had ever been. Yet even before the Scientific Revolution arose to openly challenge both Aristotle and the church, a few European thinkers had come to suspect something was wrong with the way science saw the natural world. In particular, they questioned the practice of accepting the authority of people long dead without testing their claims by experimenting and examining evidence. One of these questioners, Italian scholar Vincenzo Galilei, father of the famous Galileo Galilei, reportedly declared,

> It appears to me that those who rely simply on the weight of authority to prove any assertion, without searching out the arguments to support it, act absurdly. I wish to question freely and to answer freely without any sort of adulation [worship of ancient scholars]. That well becomes any who are sincere in the search for truth.[4]

A group of Renaissance truth seekers, known as the humanists, were in full agreement with Vincenzo about the need for modern verification of ancient scientific claims. The term "humanist" came from the Latin word for humanity. Many men, such as the Italian Petrarch and the Dutch Desiderius Erasmus, believed that it was important for humans to achieve their full potential, especially intellectually. They agreed with the ancient Greek philosophical argument that humans possess the intelligence required to uncover nature's hidden truths. They believed there was no need to turn to divine or mystical authorities to discover such truths. All that people needed to find these truths were the intellectual tools they already possessed: curiosity, reason, logic, and independent thinking.

It made no sense to Petrarch and the other humanists that people armed with such wonderful mental gifts regularly accepted the contents of centuries-old texts without question or independent verification. Most humanists worried about the accuracy of these texts. There had been no printing presses in ancient and early medieval times, so books and other writings were distributed by copying them by hand. Errors were bound to be made, and these errors would be copied, which created the opportunity for additional errors. Moreover, some humanists pointed out, the ancient texts had been translated numerous times from one language to another, a process that no doubt altered the meanings of many words and phrases. It became important to authenticate such texts, words, and phrases through observational science. That meant modern testing and reexamination of evidence. Steven Shapin wrote,

The practice of humanistic literary scholarship commonly was closely joined to that of observational science ... Observation could help decide what the original text descriptions had actually been and, further, what ancient names and descriptions referred to what existing plants [or animals]. After all, wasn't this what the ancient authorities themselves had done? Hadn't Aristotle been a close observer of the natural world?[5]

Daring to Disagree

On the eve of the Scientific Revolution, therefore, at least some European thinkers were ready to reexamine and challenge the existing state of knowledge about the natural world. The opening of the age of global exploration showed that enormous numbers of formerly unknown lands, plants, animals, and peoples existed across the globe. This fantastic realization provided still more reason to rethink existing scientific knowledge. As Europeans began to fill out their world map, some began to wonder why ancient texts—long believed to hold unending knowledge—never mentioned the American continents or the people who lived there.

These and other factors inspired a few intensely curious and brave Europeans to observe, question, and redefine the world, rather than simply to accept what they had been told about it. They advocated testing various theories by getting their hands dirty while studying nature and the world, rather than simply discussing it as philosophers would. What these pioneers of modern science did not foresee, however, was that their investigations of the world would change it beyond their wildest dreams.

CHAPTER TWO

THE COPERNICAN REVOLUTION

R ome was not built in a day, and neither was the Scientific Revolution. When Copernicus published *On the Revolutions of the Heavenly Spheres* in 1543, there was no immediate collective revelation and revolt against the existing opinions. It took about a century and a half after the publication of the book before enough Europeans accepted the heliocentric (sun-centered) theory as fact, and this period became known as the Copernican Revolution. Among the small number of scientists who gave Copernicus's theories any thought were such astronomers as Galileo Galilei, Tycho Brahe, and Johannes Kepler. These men brought the heliocentric model to the attention of the general public and permanently changed the way humans perceived the universe.

A Budding Astronomer

Nicolaus Copernicus was raised a devout Christian. It had never been his explicit intention to completely rock the foundations of Western thought and openly challenge the authority of the Catholic Church. After his father died, Copernicus's uncle, an influential bishop, made arrangements for him to study for a career in the church. Copernicus, however, was too intellectually restless to commit himself to a job and life that limited him to traditional thinking. While attending Poland's University of Krakow, he came under the wing of a mathematics professor named Albert Brudzewski. Brudzewski introduced Copernicus to contemporary astronomy, which quickly became his passion. Copernicus's introduction to and theories about the heliocentric view of the universe occurred on his own time, however, and were not the result of influence from his professors. At the university, he was trained in the

NICOLAI CO
PERNICI TORINENSIS
DE REVOLVTIONIBVS ORBI-
um coelestium, Libri VI.

Habes in hoc opere iam recens nato, & ædíto,
studiose lector, Motus stellarum, tam fixarum,
quàm erraticarum, cum ex ueteribus, tum etiam
ex recentibus obseruationibus restitutos: & no-
uis insuper ac admirabilibus hypothesibus or-
natos. Habes etiam Tabulas expeditissimas, ex
quibus eosdem ad quoduis tempus quàm facilli
me calculare poteris. Igitur eme, lege, fruere.

Ἀγεωμέτρητος ἀδεὶς εἰσίτω.

Norimbergæ apud Ioh. Petreium,
Anno M. D. XLIII.

Shown here is the title page of On the Revolutions of the Heavenly Spheres.

fundamentals of astronomy, including the use of observational tools, but these basic ideas were based on Aristotle's ancient texts, which contained many outdated theories.

Aristotle and the Greeks were not wrong about everything—they were correct in their theory that Earth is round. One strong piece of proof for this, Aristotle argued, was the fact that Earth casts a curved shadow onto the moon during lunar eclipses. However, another important aspect of his and Ptolemy's view of the cosmos was extremely incorrect. They believed that Earth rests, unmoving, at the center of the heavens. According to Aristotle (who agreed with the Pythagoreans on this point), the cosmos was made up of several large, invisible spheres that were concentric, or nested within one another. Attached to the surface of each sphere, he claimed, was a planet or other heavenly body. The sun rested on one sphere, the moon on another, Jupiter on still another, and so forth. Because these spheres were perfectly circular, according to the theory, they carried the heavenly bodies in perfect circles around the central Earth.

The Center of the Universe

The more Copernicus thought about this system of invisible concentric spheres, the more he doubted it. Among his many objections was that to hold in place all of the heavenly bodies visible in the sky, there would have to be an excessive number of these spheres, which would make the cosmos cluttered and unnecessarily complex. He also argued that the movement of these spheres, along with the entire cosmos, around Earth every 24 hours was simply not credible. For something as huge as the universe to attain this feat, he said, it would need to be moving at an unbelievably high speed. The Aristotelians had claimed that "beyond the heavens there isn't any body or place or void or anything at all," but Copernicus countered that "it is rather surprising that [the heavens] can be held together by nothing."[6]

It made much more sense to Copernicus for the opposite of the traditional view to be true: a tiny Earth moving within a huge, stationary cosmos. Copernicus determined that Earth was moving through the cosmos in a roughly circular motion. The visual and mathematical evidence indicated it was one of several planets, all of which were orbiting the stationary sun. His final conclusion, which made him famous, was that the sun was the true center of the universe. To those that doubted his findings, he asked,

Why ... should we hesitate any longer to grant to [Earth] the movement which accords naturally with its form, rather than put the whole [heavens] in a commotion—the world whose limits we do not and

A ROUND EARTH

In *On the Revolutions of the Heavenly Spheres,* Copernicus offered huge amounts of mathematical and logical evidence in support of the heliocentric theory. He began the work by stating some obvious characteristics of Earth and the heavens. In the following excerpt, for example, he presents some of the evidence proving Earth is a sphere:

> The Earth is globe-shaped ... That is made clear in this way. For when people journey northward from anywhere, the northern [point] of the axis of daily revolution gradually moves overhead, and the other [axis] moves downward to the same extent; and many stars situated to the north are seen not to [disappear], and many to the south are seen not to [appear] any more. So Italy does not see [the star] Canopus, which is visible to Egypt. And Italy sees the last star of Fluvius, which is not visible to [other regions].[1]

1. Nicolaus Copernicus, *On the Revolutions of the Heavenly Spheres,* Charles Glenn Wallis, trans. Amherst, NY: Prometheus Books, 1995, p. 9.

cannot know? And why not admit that the appearance of daily [rotation] belongs to the heavens but the reality belongs to the Earth? ... In the case of the movement of the Earth ... the whole world should be believed to be moving in a circle.[7]

Copernicus did recognize that he was not the first person to conceive of a heliocentric universe. In the 1400s, a churchman named Nicholas of Cusa had suggested that Earth moved through the heavens. All of these late medieval researchers, like Copernicus, were aware that Aristarchus had proposed a heliocentric theory in ancient times. In fact, in an early draft of *On the Revolutions of the Heavenly Spheres,* Copernicus credited Aristarchus. Yet none of these forerunners of Copernicus had presented any robust mathematical proof for their claims. As scholar Thomas S. Kuhn pointed out, Copernicus was the first to accomplish that complex and impressive feat:

> *The earth's motion [around the sun] had never been a popular concept, but by the sixteenth century it was scarcely unprecedented. What was unprecedented was the mathematical system that Copernicus built*

net, in quo terram cum orbe lunari tanquam epicyclo contineri diximus. Quinto loco Venus nono menſe reducitur. Sextum deniɋ locum Mercurius tenet, octuaginta dierum ſpacio circū currens. In medio uero omnium reſidet Sol. Quis enim in hoc

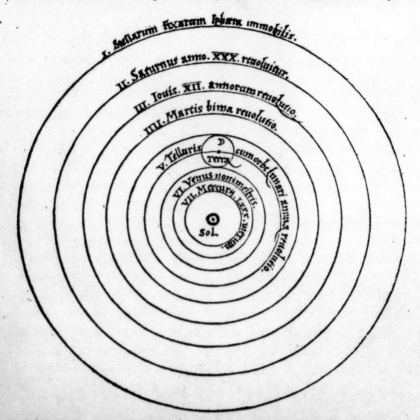

pulcherrimo templolampadem hanc in alio uel meliori loco po neret, quàm unde totum ſimul poſsit illuminare? Siquidem non inepte quidam lucernam mundi, alɳ mentem, alɳ rectorem uo= cant. Trimegiſtus uiſibilem Deum, Sophoclis Electra intuentē omnia. Ita profecto tanquam in ſolio re gali Sol reſidens circum agentem gubernat Aſtrorum familiam. Tellus quoɋ minime fraudatur lunari miniſterio , ſed ut Ariſtoteles de animalibus ait, maximā Luna cū terra cognatione habet. Concipit interea à Sole terra , & impregnatur annuo partu. Inuenimus igitur ſub hac

Copernicus argued that Earth revolved around the sun in a circular path such as those shown here.

upon the earth's motion. With the possible exception of Aristarchus, Copernicus was the first to realize that the earth's motion might solve an existing ... scientific problem ... [Copernicus] was the first to develop a detailed account of the astronomical consequences of the earth's motion. Copernicus' mathematics distinguish him from his predecessors, and it was in part because of the mathematics that his work [began] a revolution as theirs had not.[8]

Challening the Church

Unfortunately, Copernicus did not live long enough to see much of the Scientific Revolution. He died the same year his book was published, which affected the way scholars and other educated individuals viewed it. The fact that the author was not around to explain and defend its contents was one of the reasons it was so slow to change Europe's intellectual landscape. Even more influential in discouraging wide acceptance of Copernicus's explanation of the heliocentric system was the Catholic Church. For a long time, church officials had loudly backed the Aristotelian vision of the heavens because its geocentric system agreed with various statements found in the Bible. Any book that claimed Earth moved around the sun—and thus directly opposed scripture—was seen as a threat to the church's credibility. Church astronomers ridiculed and condemned Copernicus and his book. Several non-religious astronomers did likewise, hoping to gain favor with society's most powerful and influential institution. Eventually, the church banned the book.

Those astronomers and philosophers who agreed with Copernicus kept their opinions private, fearing that the church would condemn, and maybe even punish, them if they came out in support of the heliocentric system. Among these secret Copernicans was the young Italian scientist Galileo Galilei. In 1597, Galileo admitted his belief in the heliocentric system to the German astronomer and mathematician Johannes Kepler, who also agreed with most of Copernicus's ideas. Galileo, like many scientists who believed in Copernicus, was too frightened to publicly advocate for the heliocentric theory because he feared that Catholic leaders would ruin his life and his family name.

Support and Punishment

Supporters of Copernicus such as Galileo had good reason to want to keep their true scientific views a secret. In 1600, an Italian scientist, Giordano Bruno, went public with his support for Copernicus's views. In the early 1580s, Bruno had moved to London, where the church could not have him arrested

HERESIES AND ERRORS

The Catholic Church banned *On the Revolutions of the Heavenly Spheres* in 1616. In that same year, the church issued a statement on the growing scientific support for Copernicus:

> *In regard to several books containing various heresies and errors, to prevent the emergence of more serious harm throughout Christendom, the Holy Congregation of the Most Illustrious Lord Cardinals in charge of the Index [of banned books] has decided that they should be altogether condemned and prohibited ... wherever and in whatever language they are printed or about to be printed. It orders that henceforth no one, of whatever station or condition, should dare print them, or have them printed, or read them, or have them in one's possession in any way.*[1]

1. Quoted in Maurice A. Finocchiaro, trans., *The Essential Galileo.* Indianapolis, IN: Hackett Publishing Company, 2008, p. 176.

Pope Paul V was the head of the Catholic Church when Copernicus's book was banned.

because England had recently broken away from the Catholic Church and become Protestant. There, he had published two essays supporting the heliocentric theory: "The Ash Wednesday Supper" and "On the Infinite Universe and Worlds."

These works made some logical, but radical, leaps based on Copernicus's ideas. One stated that there were other planets like Earth orbiting other stars like the sun, and there might even be intelligent creatures living on those faraway planets.

Galileo was eventually forced to defend himself before Catholic officials, as shown here, for supporting the heliocentric theory.

Bruno wrote,

Our world, called the terrestrial globe, is identical as far as material composition goes with the other worlds, the [orbiting] bodies of other stars ... it is childish to have believed or believe otherwise. [On distant planets] there live and strive ... many and innumerable simple and composite individuals to no less extent than we see these living and growing on the back of this [our globe] ... Aristotle and others are blinded so as not to perceive the motion of the earth to be true and necessary. They are, indeed, so inhibited that they cannot believe this [the motion of the earth] to be possible.[9]

Church officials desperately wanted to silence Bruno for publicly stating what they claimed were heretical ideas, but as long as he stayed in England, he was safe. In 1591, however, Bruno made a big mistake. Thinking he was keeping a low profile, he paid a visit to the Italian city of Venice. There, Bruno was arrested, imprisoned in Rome, and tried as a heretic. When he continually refused to abandon his views, the church burned him at the stake.

Bruno's sad fate was a warning that it was not yet safe for most European scientists to publicly support the heliocentric theory. However, that did not mean one could not challenge Aristotle. In 1588, the Danish astronomer

Though Giordano Bruno was killed, he is remembered through monuments such as this.

HOLDING BACK

In 1597, Galileo wrote a letter to noted German astronomer Johannes Kepler to explain why he had not gone public with his support of the heliocentric theory:

> Like you, I accepted the Copernican position several years ago and discovered from thence the causes of many natural effects which are doubtless inexplicable by the current theories. I have written up many reasons and refutations on the subject, but I have not dared until now to bring them into the open, being warned by the fortunes of Copernicus himself ... who procured for himself immortal fame among a few but stepped down among the great crowd (for this is how foolish people are numbered), only to be derided and dishonored. I would dare publish my thoughts if there were many like you; but, since there are not, I shall forebear [hold back].[1]

1. Quoted in Giorgio de Santillana, *The Crime of Galileo*. Chicago, IL: University of Chicago Press, 1955, p. 11.

Tycho Brahe showed that there was a middle ground—a way to say that Aristotle had made a mistake without contradicting the Bible and angering the church. In his new model, all the planets except for Earth revolved in perfect circles around the sun. Meanwhile, the sun moved, carrying those bodies with it, around a stationary Earth. Sure enough, church leaders had few complaints about Brahe's cosmic view because it was essentially geocentric and therefore no threat to prevailing religious beliefs. The only problem was that it was incorrect.

Machinery of the Heavens

Tycho Brahe made it possible for the Copernican system, which he had rejected, to eventually triumph. Brahe had heard good things about a young German mathematics teacher, Johannes Kepler, and offered him a job. Over the course of two decades, Brahe had closely observed the planets and collected an enormous amount of information about their motions. He was confident that careful studies of this data would show the shapes of the planets' orbits and prove that his model was correct. Kepler's assigned task, which began around 1600, was to use complex mathematical formulas to make sense of the collected data, but things did not work out the way Brahe expected.

Johannes Kepler discovered that planets orbit the sun in elliptical shapes.

He grew ill and died in 1601 and left Kepler in the middle of decoding his data. The work continued for several years, during which the young mathematician tried over and over to make Brahe's figures match the perfect circles he and other scientists assumed for the planetary orbits. However, no matter how hard he tried, the data simply did not match such orbits. This caused Kepler to consider that he and all his predecessors, including Copernicus, might have been wrong: What if the orbits of the planets were not circular, but oval-shaped? When Kepler plugged Brahe's data into these modified orbits, everything matched precisely.

In 1609, Kepler published the first two of his three planetary laws. The first one stated that the planets travel in elliptical orbits around the sun. The second law stated that a planet picks up speed as it nears the sun and slows down as it moves away from it. As a result, an imaginary line connecting a planet to the sun sweeps out equal areas in equal amounts of time. A few years later, Kepler announced his third law, which connected a planet's period, or the time it takes to orbit the sun, to its distance from the sun. Because Mars is farther from the sun than Earth is, Kepler argued, Mars moves more slowly than Earth and therefore has a longer period. Because Kepler's laws showed how the planets' visible movements could be explained in terms of their revolutions around the sun, they provided extremely persuasive proof for the heliocentric theory. They perfectly explained the moon's orbit around Earth and even the orbits of all the comets that had been observed by astronomers.

Kepler was certain that his discoveries would revolutionize astronomy, in part by showing that Copernicus was right. In his 1619 book *The Harmony of the Worlds*, Kepler wrote that he wanted his discoveries to open a new chapter in the history of astronomy. Though he directly opposed the Catholic view of the universe with his theories, he argued that his new knowledge was a gift from God and should be treated with respect by the church.

In spite of the mathematical evidence Kepler had provided, the Copernican Revolution was not yet complete. The church, along with a number of scientists who dared not defy its authority, continued to resist the heliocentric system. The math Kepler had employed was complex, and few people could understand it. What the field of astronomy needed was proof everyone could easily understand. Even before Kepler's death in 1630, a new invention—the telescope—was the perfect means to provide that proof. The only question was whether those who were most resistant to intellectual change would believe the evidence of their own eyes.

CHapTer THree

FAR-SEEING

As Kepler published his work and the Scientific Revolution continued to progress, astronomers kept their eyes on the sky—literally. The actual inventor of the instrument called a telescope is unknown; the earliest patent for a similar device was submitted in 1608 in the Netherlands. The word spread through Europe until it reached Galileo and he built his own version in 1609, but there had been attempts long before then to create a long-distance looking glass. Telescopes allow users to see very far distances into space by collecting electromagnetic radiation, or visible light, using mirrors. The word "telescope" comes from the ancient Greek word meaning "far-seeing." For the first time, humans did not have to rely on their imaginations when considering the stars—and it could only get better:

> From the early seventeenth century, observers using telescopes ... suggested that even more details and more marvels awaited only improved instruments ... Who could confidently say what did and did not exist in the world when tomorrow might reveal as yet undreamed inhabitants in the domains of the very distant.[10]

The telescope seemed miraculous. It would surely be hard for anyone to argue against what they could see with their own eyes. However, the Catholic Church once again grew suspicious and distrustful of new information and practices that they themselves had not approved; new discoveries might distract faithful followers from the church's absolute authority. The church quickly punished Galileo for the construction of his telescope in hopes of beating back the advancing forces of science, and while the church succeeded initially, the revolution was too powerful to stop.

Shown here is an early telescope.

Naked-Eye Astronomy

Historians now refer to the era of space study before the telescope was invented as naked-eyed astronomy. This period covered time from thousands of years before Galileo in 1609, including the eras of the ancient Babylonians, Persians, Chinese, and Greeks. When the church argued that a strong tradition of astronomy had already been established, it invoked the authority of the whole of history.

Naked-eye astronomy happened in a time before light pollution, so although it may seem amateur by today's standards, much of the night sky was visible to these scientists, and they kept detailed records of what they observed. By Europe's last few medieval centuries, naked-eye astronomy had reached a remarkable level of technical sophistication. Kings and nobles poured large amounts of money into building observatories where astronomers studied the heavens. This trend reached its height in Denmark in the 16th century. In 1576, King Frederick II agreed to give Tycho Brahe all the financial backing he required for his work. Brahe acquired a castle equipped with a large observatory, along with dozens of assistants and servants. Frederick told Brahe, "There you can live peacefully and carry out the studies that interest you, without anyone disturbing you ... I will sail over to the island from time to time and see your work in astronomy and chemistry, and gladly support your investigations."[11]

The observatory on the island had a large central room filled with books, star charts, and many mechanical instruments, including an armillary sphere. This old astronomical device consists of several large, movable metal rings with numbers painted onto their edges. These numbers represented the 180 degrees into which the visible sky was divided. By moving the armillary sphere's rings in various ways, Brahe and his assistants were able to measure the positions of stars and planets at any given time and with amazing precision. One of the armillary spheres Brahe built was 10 feet (3 meters) across and could measure star positions to within a fraction of a degree—an incredibly tiny margin of error for an instrument guided solely by the naked eye.

On one evening in November 1577, Brahe saw a bright object in the western sky that immediately got his attention. It was fuzzy looking and had a faint tail. Clearly, he reasoned, the object was a comet. He vigilantly watched it move across the sky from night to night until it vanished from view in early 1578. After carefully studying the measurements his instruments had made of the object, he became perplexed. The comet appeared to have been located well beyond the moon, but this sounded impossible. Aristotle had insisted that comets always move inside Earth's

Tycho Brahe came up with a theory that combined heliocentrism and geocentrism, shown here.

atmosphere. Brahe's instruments had indicated that the comet was orbiting the sun, and Aristotle had said that all heavenly bodies, including the sun, move around Earth. In this way, using only naked-eye observations, Brahe was able to disprove Aristotle's theory. The astronomer's observations of the comet of 1577 became his main motivation in constructing his new model of the cosmos, in which all the heavenly bodies except Earth orbited the sun, while the sun moved around Earth.

The Birth of the Scope

In the 1570s and 1580s, it appeared to most people, including church leaders, that astronomy had reached its greatest possible height. No one could imagine what an instrument like the telescope might be capable of. Although historians do not know who invented the telescope originally, they do know of some of the first versions that were created. One of these was reportedly built by English mathematician and surveyor Leonard Digges. Remarks made in the letters of his son, Thomas, and others who knew him suggest that Digges made two or more scopes sometime in the 1550s. Evidence implies that they were of both types of telescopes—refractors and reflectors. (Other kinds of scopes, some of which combine elements of refractors and reflectors, did not begin to appear until the 1800s.) A refractor creates a magnified image by passing light through two convex lenses, which are thicker in the middle and thinner toward the edges. A reflector creates a similar image by bouncing light off of a concave mirror, or one that is thinner in the middle and wider at the edges. (In Digges's era, the word "telescope" had not yet been coined. Experts on optics—the study of the behavior of light—at the time referred to refracting scopes as perspective glasses and called the mirror of a reflecting scope a plain glass.)

The strongest single piece of evidence for Digges's scopes is an official English government report made around 1580. Evidently, Leonard and Thomas Digges wanted to keep their telescopes a secret. The reasons for this are unclear; it may be that they feared others would steal the design, causing them to lose both control of the invention and any money they might have made from selling it, but word of the scopes leaked out. Eventually, a major adviser to Queen Elizabeth I heard a rumor that the Digges family had a device that made faraway objects appear to be closer. Interested in the military potential of such an instrument, the adviser sent an agent named William Bourne to see if there was any truth to the rumor. Bourne's surviving report, though undetailed and unreliable for some historians, seems to describe both reflecting and refracting telescopes with some degree of accuracy.

By the 1580s, the Diggeses' scopes were hidden so well that record of them disappeared. By that time, eyeglass makers in various parts of Europe were experimenting with lenses in ways that made the independent invention of the telescope inevitable. (These craftsmen had been using convex lenses to help people with vision problems since the late 1200s.) One spectacle maker, a Dutchman named Hans Lippershey, tinkered together a small but workable refractor in 1608. It consisted of two convex lenses, later called the objective and secondary lenses. The objective lens collected incoming light and bent, or refracted, it, focusing it into a small image. The secondary lens, which Lippershey placed in front of the objective, magnified the image, making it look larger and closer. To Lippershey and his associates, the small scope, which he called a spyglass, was at first viewed mainly as a novelty. Eventually, Lippershey, like Queen Elizabeth's adviser, realized that his device might also have military applications, including allowing commanders to see enemies approaching from a great distance. Late in 1608, he gave the invention to the Dutch government.

The Moons of Jupiter

What Lippershey did not anticipate was that rumors of his spyglasses

MEASURING THE ALTITUDE OF A STAR

Tycho Brahe employed numerous instruments to aid him in observing the night sky and measuring the positions of the heavenly bodies. Among these devices were quadrants he designed himself. At the time, a quadrant measured the altitude of a star or planet from the horizon. It was an apparatus with a wooden or metal framework shaped like a large triangle and covered 90 degrees, or a quarter of a full circle. To use one of his quadrants, Brahe sighted two distant objects through holes on the device's rim and measured the angle between them. The degree of accuracy he achieved in doing this often amazes people today. Using his complex calculations, he could measure some star positions within an error range of less than 1 percent of a degree.

had already spread across Europe. Hearing about a seemingly magical looking device made with lenses, several intelligent individuals immediately set to work experimenting with lenses and building their own scopes, including Italian Paolo Sarpi and English Thomas Harriot. Another clever Italian, Galileo Galilei, heard about the Dutch invention in 1609. Putting everything else aside, he hurriedly obtained some convex lenses and began trying them out in various combinations. Although he had never seen an example of Lippershey's spyglass, he grasped the principle involved. After working with the lenses, he was able to create a telescope that magnified objects to be 10 times larger. This early scope magnified images about as well as an average pair of modern binoculars. Galileo took the instrument to Venice and demonstrated it for the members of that city's leadership, who immediately recognized its military potential. The demonstration was also intended to establish Galileo as a major telescope builder and cutting-edge astronomer.

The Venetian rulers, along with nearly everyone else who had built or seen previous telescopes, completely overlooked the device's potential for viewing the moon, the planets, and other objects in the sky. Being an astronomer, however, Galileo appreciated this potential. As soon as he returned home from Venice, where he had given his first scope to that city's leader, he built a new instrument that magnified objects even more and pointed it toward the moon. To his delight, he saw that it was covered with craters, mountains, and what appeared to be seas.

Hans Lippershey was a spectacle maker who made multiple versions of a spyglass.

(Later astronomers discovered that instead of bodies of water, the formations he saw were actually large plains of dust.)

Barely able to contain his excitement, Galileo pointed the scope at various spots in the Milky Way, the long band of pale light that ripples through several constellations. The instrument revealed that the seemingly solid smudge in the night sky was made up of countless individual stars, nearly all of them too distant to see with the unaided eye. Switching to the planets Venus, Jupiter, and Mars, Galileo saw globes that looked like the moon, only smaller (because they are much farther from Earth than the moon is).

Most important, for both astronomy and the Scientific Revolution, was something Galileo saw near Jupiter's globe. At first he thought they were four distant stars that happened to lie in the planet's present line of sight, but as he observed them over the following nights, he saw that they moved. The movement was not random, but showed that the four objects were orbiting Jupiter, exactly as the moon revolves around Earth. Realizing that he was seeing Jupiter's own moons, Galileo immediately grasped the momentous implication this discovery had for the ongoing Copernican Revolution. Scholar James MacLachlan explained that, "up to this time, Aristotelians had argued that the earth was the center of the universe because everything seemed to revolve around it, and no other object was the center of any rotations. Now, with moons in orbit around Jupiter, that argument was clearly invalid."[12]

Plainly, Galileo realized, Earth was not the center of all things, as both the ancient sages and the church's leaders had long thought. The geocentric theory was wrong. In Galileo's mind, the proof for this major assertion was now inarguable. The telescope provided tangible evidence that anyone, even someone with no scientific background at all, could see as conclusive. Thus, he reasoned, he no longer had to fear what the church would do when its leaders found out about his astronomical views. They would have no choice but to believe the evidence of their own eyes and alter their views about the cosmos accordingly.

Galileo compiled his telescopic discoveries in writing and published them in a booklet in 1610 titled *The Starry Messenger*. Its author was thrilled when the Latin edition of the book rapidly sold out and was subsequently translated into numerous other languages. Soon, Galileo was famous throughout Europe and beyond. This notoriety brought him job offers in his native Italy. Cosimo II, grand duke of Tuscany, supported his research and encouraged him to continue experimenting. Galileo also accepted a

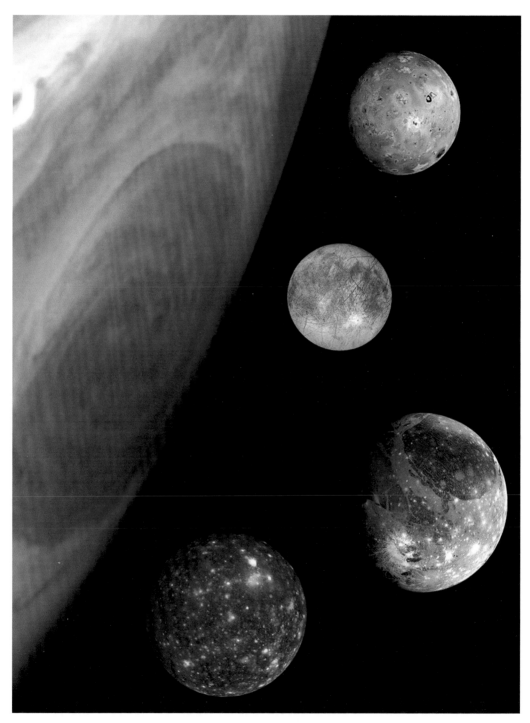

Seeing Jupiter's moons in orbit convinced Galileo that he had proof that Earth was not the center of the universe.

MORE ERRORS AND HERESIES

E ven after the telescope provided visual proof that the sun was the center of the universe, Galileo was forced to publicly admit that he had been wrong when he advocated ideas that went against what the church taught. Forced by the church, he issued a statement in which he admitted heresy and took back all his ideas:

> [I admit] that I must altogether abandon the false opinion that the Sun is the center of the world and immovable and that the Earth is not the center of the world and moves and that I must not hold, defend, or teach in any way whatsoever, verbally or in writing, the said false doctrine, and after [the church] notified to me that the said doctrine was contrary to Holy Scripture—I wrote and printed a book in which I discuss this new doctrine already condemned ... I have been pronounced by the [church] to be vehemently suspected of heresy, that is to say, of having held and believed that the Sun is the center of the world and immovable and that the Earth is not at the center and moves. Therefore, desiring to remove from the minds of ... all faithful Christians, this vehement suspicion justly conceived against me, with sincere heart and [true] faith I abjure, curse, and detest the aforesaid errors and heresies.[1]

1. Quoted in Wade Rowland, *Galileo's Mistake: A New Look at the Epic Confrontation Between Galileo and the Church*. New York, NY: Skyhorse Publishing, 2003. PDF e-book.

professorship at the University of Pisa in northern Italy.

Men Stretch Out Their Eyes

Galileo's joyful discovery eventually turned to distress. His assumption that church officials would be persuaded to change their views about the heavens based on what the telescope had revealed turned out to be wrong. In fact, to his astonishment, he found that many people—both inside and outside the church—would not accept the telescopic evidence. Some even refused to look into the device. Those church officials who did look through the telescope and saw Jupiter's moons told Galileo that this, and other so-called evidence the instrument had revealed, proved nothing. It all could be explained, they said, using Brahe's model of the heavens, which was partially geocentric. In 1616, they warned Galileo not to write anything else suggesting the Copernican theory might be correct.

In 1623, the astronomer met several times with his friend Pope Urban VIII in Rome. Galileo walked away from the meetings with the impression that he could write about the Copernican view—as long as he made it very clear that it was only a hypothesis. He got to work on a major treatise titled *Dialogue Concerning the Two Chief World Systems: Ptolemaic and Copernican*, which he published in 1632. At first, the church cleared the book for publication, but shortly after it was released to the public, the church changed its mind, halted further publication, and ordered Galileo to stand trial on suspicion of heresy. The proceedings did not go well for the scientist. In 1633, Galileo was found guilty and forced to publicly renounce the heliocentric theory. After this humiliation, he endured the constraints of house arrest until he died in 1642 as an unhappy man. In the end, however, Galileo was proven correct. In the century following his death, science and astronomy advanced rapidly. It became clear that the heliocentric view of the cosmos was correct, and it was repeatedly proven through continuing advances in optics and telescope making. Refractors got larger and showed increasingly sharp images, which clarified various cosmic mysteries. Galileo's small, relatively crude scope revealed Saturn as a fuzzy blob with bumps protruding from its sides, but in 1655, Dutch astronomer Christiaan Huygens observed Saturn with a larger, more refined instrument. It showed that the bumps Galileo had seen were actually the outer edges of that planet's ring system.

Scientists experimented with new telescope designs, including ways of building effective reflectors. In the late 1600s, English researcher Isaac Newton—who is considered one of the most brilliant individuals to have ever lived—constructed a new working reflector. In 1669, Newton wrote to a friend and declared that he had used his device to get a clear picture of Jupiter and its moons. Newton proceeded to create a second reflector, which he gave to the recently formed Royal Society—a group of scientists dedicated to the advancement of knowledge. That advancement continued and accelerated as telescopes became more sophisticated. In the late 1700s, German-born English astronomer William Herschel built several large reflectors, and with one of them, he discovered Uranus, the first new planet found since ancient times.

By Herschel's day, the Scientific Revolution had brought enormous changes in the way people viewed the universe, nature, and the quest to better understand both. The arrogant old notion—that nothing new about the heavens would ever be found—had been swept away. In its place was a much more optimistic vision of the future, in which the discoveries made by the human mind, aided

William Herschel, shown here, discovered Uranus with a large telescope.

by increasingly effective technology, could be limitless. Christopher Wren, the famous English architect who was also an astronomer and physicist, summed it up:

A time [will] come when men should be able to stretch out their eyes, as snails do, and extend them fifty feet in length; by which means they should be able to discover two thousand times as many stars as we can; and find the galaxy to [include many] of them; and every [indistinct] star appearing as if it were the [ground] of some other world, at an incomprehensible distance, bury'd in the vast abyss of [space].[13]

CHAPTER FOUR

THE SCIENTIFIC METHOD

Though it experienced especially massive advances, astronomy was far from the only field of science that was progressing during the Scientific Revolution. Scientists who were keeping their eyes on Earth were realizing that there was a need for a scientific method. The scientific method, as it is understood today, is a set of rules and techniques that are used to investigate new knowledge, often by experimentation. Up until the Scientific Revolution, however, there was no set of rules that was accepted by the entire science community. Most individual scientists had their own ways of conducting research. When the Scientific Revolution brought together all of the best aspects of scientific methodology, a new way to conduct research was established—and it is still in use today.

First Principles

A major part of the process of creating a scientific method during the 1500s, 1600s, and 1700s was looking back on what earlier thinkers had done and either keeping or rejecting their ideas and approaches. It was (and still is) difficult to conclude who had been the first person to propose a version of the scientific method. It is possible that several people did so independently in different places and times. One of the earliest known examples was the unknown author of an ancient Egyptian medical book now known as the Edwin Smith Papyrus. Dating to about 1600 BC, it advocated that a doctor follow a series of logical steps in trying to heal a patient. These included examination, diagnosis, treatment, and prognosis. This organized method for dealing with disease is nearly identical to the one used by modern physicians, but not all Egyptian doctors followed this process. Other approaches to healing existed in ancient Egypt, many of which relied on superstition rather than logic.

STARTING WITH THE FACTS

Aristotle believed that one of the first and most basic steps in making correct statements about nature or the world was to study what others had said before on the subject and then forming an opinion based on given facts. In the opening of his essay "Posterior Analytics," he wrote,

> All teaching and all intellectual learning come about from already existing knowledge. This is evident if we consider it in every case; for the mathematical sciences are acquired in this fashion, and so is each of the other arts. And similarly too with arguments ... [They] produce their teaching through what we are already aware of ... getting their [principles] from men who grasp them.[1]

1. Aristotle, "Posterior Analytics" in *The Complete Works of Aristotle*, Vol. 1, Jonathan Barnes, ed. Princeton, NJ: Princeton University Press, 2014, p. 114.

When Galileo and other researchers of the Scientific Revolution were born, the chief method of assessing new knowledge was the one created by Aristotle in the fourth century BC. Aristotle believed that all knowledge could be traced back to a basic and eternal set of what he called first principles. These were fundamental truths about nature that did not need to be questioned. One could accept these truths through beliefs that had long existed, as well as by assumptions based on simple observation. For example, based on observation, it appeared that the heavenly bodies moved around a stationary Earth, so it seemed only right that Earth should be the center of all things. That fact could be accepted as a first principle. Another Aristotelian first principle derived from a general belief in higher powers. Most people accepted that the heavenly system called the cosmos had been created by a god or gods, and it seemed to make no sense for a divine being to fashion an imperfect system. Therefore, it could be accepted that the universe operated on perfect principles. One such principle was that the moon and other heavenly bodies followed perfectly circular paths around Earth. According to Aristotle, any new proposal that contradicted such first principles was automatically incorrect.

Aristotle also believed that various scientific principles could be derived through logic, and he devised a complex system to prove it. The system

A MORE PERFECT
USE OF THE HUMAN MIND

Francis Bacon, a famous philosopher and author in the late 16th and early 17th centuries, acknowledged that ancient thinkers, such as Aristotle, had contributed a lot to human knowledge. However, he felt that their ideas should not always be automatically accepted without further testing, because the world had changed a great deal since ancient times. In his *The Great Instauration*, published in 1620, Bacon wrote,

> We have no reason to be ashamed of the discoveries which have been made, and no doubt the ancients proved themselves in everything that turns on wit and abstract meditation, wonderful men. But, as in former ages, when men sailed only by observation of the stars, they could indeed coast along the shores of the old continent or cross a few small and Mediterranean seas; but before the ocean could be traversed and the new world discovered, the use of the mariner's needle [compass], as a more faithful and certain guide, had to be found out; in like manner ... before we can reach the remoter and more hidden parts of nature, it is necessary that a more perfect use and application of the human mind and intellect be introduced.[1]

1. Francis Bacon, *The Great Instauration*. New York, NY: Simon and Schuster, 2012. PDF e-book.

utilized a method called a syllogism, which operates by comparing one thing to another and making conclusions based on that comparison. Typically, syllogistic arguments use a standard A, B, therefore C structure. One example of such a syllogism would be:

A: All people breathe.
B: All children are people.
Therefore C: All children breathe.

Aristotle believed that syllogisms could be used in other ways as well. For instance, if A does something, and B does not do that thing, then the conclusion, C, is that A is not B. An example of this might be:

A: Dogs bark.
B: Goats do not bark.
Therefore C: Dogs and goats are not the same.

In all his theories, Aristotle emphasized the power of observation and reason to make scientific and other conclusions, but he did not advocate for experimentation, nor did most other Greek thinkers. As scholar H. D. P. Lee explained, this was a fundamental weakness in their scientific method:

> The comparative failure of the Greeks to develop experimental science was due to many causes ... They lacked instruments of precision—there were, for instance, no accurate clocks until Galileo discovered the pendulum. They did not produce until a comparatively late date any glass suitable for chemical experiment or lens-making. Their iron-making technique was [basic], which [prevented] the development of the machine. Their mathematical notation was clumsy and unsuited to scientific calculation. All these things would have severely limited the development of an experimental science if the Greeks fully grasped its method. But the experimental method eluded them. They observed but they did not experiment.[14]

Muslim Scientific Advancement

Even in the 21st century, many textbooks in Western countries fail to mention that scholars in the Scientific Revolution were often influenced by medieval Arab Muslim scientists who preceded them by several centuries. Beginning in the 800s, well before the works of Aristotle and many other Greeks were rediscovered in Europe, Muslim scholars translated those Greek texts into Arabic. At the House of Wisdom in Baghdad (in what is now Iraq), Muslim scholars wrote commentaries on the Greek books. Inspired by these works, the Muslim scholars went on to produce a burst of scientific accomplishments of their own. A mathematician named Muhammad ibn Musa al-Khwarizmi was the first to introduce what came to be called Arabic numerals. These were based on an Indian number system. Because of their simplicity, these numbers made mathematical calculation considerably easier than it had been in the past. Arabic numerals were introduced into Europe beginning in the late 900s and subsequently improved the methodology of scientists across Asia and Europe. Arabic numerals are still in use across most of the world today.

Arab Muslim scholars made many other contributions to science, including in the disciplines of medicine, chemistry, geography, astronomy, and cartography (mapmaking). Perhaps the greatest of these were the achievements of Ibn al-Haytham, who was born in 965 in Iraq and educated in Baghdad. He studied several topics, but his main interest was the behavior of light. He was the first person to correctly describe how people see objects, and today he is

Al-Khwarizmi developed Arabic numerals, which were introduced to Europe in the 900s.

universally recognized as the father of the science of optics. According to one modern researcher,

He proved experimentally ... that the so-called emission theory (which stated that light from our eyes shines upon the objects we see), which was believed by great thinkers such as Plato, Euclid and Ptolemy, was wrong and established the modern idea that we see because light enters our eyes.

What he also did that no other scientist had tried before was to use mathematics to describe and prove this process.[15]

Another crucial contribution al-Haytham made to science was to formulate a scientific method containing the concept of experimentation. Closely familiar with Aristotle's works, he greatly respected the Greek's thoughts and accomplishments. However, al-Haytham also recognized that Aristotle had proven his assertions only verbally, which meant that they could be endlessly challenged by other theories through experimentation. Performing experiments could show which theories were true and which were false. The result, as researcher Martyn Shuttleworth explained, was that al-Haytham developed a scientific method very similar to our own:

1. *State an explicit problem, based upon observation*

and experimentation.
2. *Test or criticize a hypothesis through experimentation.*
3. *Interpret the data and come to a conclusion, ideally using mathematics.*
4. *Publish the findings.*

Ibn al-Haytham, brilliantly, understood that controlled and systematic experimentation and measurement were essential to discovering new knowledge.[16]

Experimentation

In the 1100s, some of al-Haytham's texts, some works by other Muslim scientists, and books by Aristotle and other Greeks—lost to the West since Rome's fall—were finally being recognized in Europe. Interest in them was strong, and they were rapidly translated into Latin. Among the first Europeans to be strongly influenced by them was English friar and philosopher Roger Bacon in the 1200s. Among many accomplishments, Bacon played an especially prominent role in the evolution of the scientific method. Impressed by al-Haytham's ideas on methodology, he promoted the use of experimentation along with observation and logical deduction. In a work appropriately titled *On Experimental Science*, Bacon stated,

There are two ways of acquiring knowledge, one through reason, the other by experiment. Argument

Roger Bacon was among the first Europeans to advocate for the need for experimentation in science.

reaches a conclusion and compels us to admit it, but it neither makes us certain nor so annihilates doubt that the mind rests calm in the intuition of truth, unless it finds this certitude [certainty] by way of experience. Thus many have arguments toward attainable facts, but because they have not experienced them, they overlook them and neither avoid a harmful nor follow a beneficial course. Even if a man that has never seen fire, proves by good reasoning that fire burns, and devours and destroys things, nevertheless the mind of one hearing his arguments would never be convinced, nor would he avoid fire until he puts his hand or some combustible thing into it in order to prove by experiment what the argument taught. But after the fact of combustion is experienced, the mind is satisfied and lies calm in the certainty of truth. Hence argument is not enough, but experience is.[17]

Later, during the Scientific Revolution, another Englishman, Francis Bacon (no relation to Roger), also supported the use of experiments as part of scientific research. To start, he discarded the idea of accepting first principles about nature based on assumptions, a process that Aristotle had routinely used. Instead of relying on assumed knowledge, Bacon argued, one should start with observation, then move to gathering as many unbiased facts as possible about the thing being observed. Next,

one should study these facts diligently and draw one or more preliminary conclusions, or hypotheses, from them. Finally, one should devise experiments to test those conclusions. If the tests showed a conclusion was wrong, the researcher should go back to the facts and draw a new one.

Another important early modern contributor to the scientific method was French mathematician, physicist, and philosopher René Descartes. He viewed the natural world and everything within it as a massive collection of mechanical objects, like a giant machine, all carefully manufactured by God. Further, Descartes proposed, God had deliberately designed these machine parts so that humans could explain them using mathematics. The single exception was the human mind (or soul), which Descartes claimed was separate from mechanical things and blessed with a divine spark.

As for the method Descartes suggested for investigating God's vast cosmic machine, he partly echoed Aristotle. One should begin with reason and logic rather than observation, Descartes declared. However, first, one should break down the problem at hand into several smaller parts; this is because understanding each part will allow the investigator to make an overall conclusion about the whole. About this process, eventually called reductionism (because it reduced large topics into smaller ones), he instructed,

Francis Bacon, a prominent philosopher, strongly supported a push toward scientific experimentation.

AN INFORMED ESTIMATE

L ike many other scientists, Galileo used induction, which is the process of drawing conclusions based on a specific set of observations. He rightly recognized that his final conclusion would have to be only an informed estimate because of all the variables involved in most natural systems. Researcher Martyn Shuttleworth elaborated:

> He believed that it would be impossible for an experimenter to take into account every single variable. In the world of physics, for example, Galileo theorized that mass had no effect upon gravitational acceleration.
>
> No experiment could ever hope to measure this perfectly, because of air resistance, friction and inaccuracies with timing devices and methods.
>
> However, repetition by independent researchers could build up a body of evidence that allowed an extrapolation [estimation based on observations] to the general theory to be made.[1]

1. Martyn Shuttleworth, "History of the Scientific Method," Explorable.com, August 18, 2009. explorable.com/history-of-the-scientific-method.

divide each of the difficulties [one] would examine into as many parts as would be possible and as would be required in order to better resolve them ... beginning with those objects the most simple and the most easy to know, in order to ascend little by little, as by degrees, to the knowledge of the most [complex] ones.[18]

While Francis Bacon and Descartes advocated reaching final conclusions in different ways, parts of each of their methods were both valid and useful, so modern science combined their approaches. In the 21st century, it is standard procedure in science to observe; reduce the thing to be studied into small, manageable parts; draw preliminary conclusions; and perform experiments to verify those conclusions.

Superior Experimental Evidence

Galileo was also an advocate for experimentation to prove hypotheses.

Descartes believed that the human mind was the only thing that could not be explained with math.

Following his death, a story circulated widely that he had staged an experiment to refute one of Aristotle's statements about motion. Aristotle had claimed that objects of different weights fall at different rates; specifically that heavier objects fall faster than lighter ones. Galileo knew that Aristotle had not tested this hypothesis through experimentation—by physically dropping objects of varying weights—and suspected he was wrong. Galileo was certain that all objects, regardless of weight, would fall at the same rate. That much of the story is true; though he was not the first, Galileo did have this theory. However, there is a legend that Galileo dropped balls of varying weights off the Leaning Tower of Pisa to test this, and that part of the story has never been confirmed. A similar experiment was performed in 1612 by an Italian professor, who dropped two balls of different weights simultaneously from the Leaning Tower of Pisa. He reported that the larger ball beat the smaller ball to the ground by a small margin, which prompted him to claim that Aristotle was correct.

The experiment, however, actually proved Galileo right. Many years later, in *Discourses and Mathematical Demonstrations Relating to Two New Sciences*, Galileo recalled the experiment. According to Aristotle's argument, the larger object should have fallen twice as fast as the smaller one. Yet, as Galileo reminded his readers, the objects landed at nearly the same time. The tiny difference, he said, could be explained by the effects of air resistance, which were more noticeable on the smaller object. Much later, in 1971, Apollo 15 astronaut Dave Scott stood on the moon's surface and simultaneously dropped a hammer and a feather. Because the moon has no air, there was no air resistance—and sure enough, both objects touched the ground at exactly the same time.

Francis Bacon's and Galileo's use of experimentation to supplement observation and reason strongly influenced other scientists of their generation and those that followed. In the 1660s, the newly formed Royal Society followed their lead. That prestigious organization openly stated that experimental evidence was always superior and preferable to theoretical evidence. Not long afterward, Isaac Newton reaffirmed the main elements of good scientific methodology. These included careful observation and fact gathering, forming hypotheses based on observed facts, and testing hypotheses through experimentation. In this way, by the end of the Scientific Revolution in the mid-1700s, the modern scientific method had emerged. It has changed very little since.

CHAPTER FIVE

BLOOD, GERMS, AND THE MICROSCOPE

The Scientific Revolution was especially notable for bringing attention to developments in medical research. Medical research, including exploration of the workings of the human body and known diseases, had been standing still since the year 200 AD, when the Greek physician Galen died. Galen was the leading doctor of the Roman Empire because he collected and referred to all the theories and practices of the Greek doctors in the past. Galen's work was extraordinarily influential because he performed numerous experiments. He dissected pigs, dogs, and other animals. He also wrote his own books, describing the outcomes of his experiments and explaining the medical knowledge of the time. Many of these texts have survived to this day.

After Galen's death, no doctors achieved any level of medical accomplishment that could come close. His books remained the chief references for scientists and students. Just like with astronomy works, when Rome fell, Galen's books were translated into Arabic and studied by Muslims before they were rediscovered in Europe much later on. Europeans felt that no new medical research was needed, since Galen seemed to have covered it all. In the minds of many European doctors before the Scientific Revolution, Galen's books were the medical equivalent of the Bible—they were not to be questioned or improved.

With the beginning of the Scientific Revolution, however, scientists and doctors began to suspect that advancement in medical knowledge might be beneficial. Before long, one influential doctor, Andreas Vesalius, and his students realized that anatomy (the structure of the human body) was a science that was not exhausted—it fact, it had barely

The Greek doctor Galen wrote books that were respected for more than 1,000 years.

even been explored. With the help of a groundbreaking new tool—the microscope—many new discoveries were on their way.

Human Dissection

Vesalius, a Belgian, was born in 1514. After studying anatomy in Paris, he journeyed to Padua, Italy, to complete his education in 1537. There, he witnessed doctors doing dissections of human corpses, something that Galen had not been able to do because the laws of his time prohibited it. When Vesalius started doing his own human dissections, he quickly concluded that human anatomy was improperly and inaccurately taught, not only in Paris and Padua, but all across Europe. John Gribbin explained,

> The teaching (such as it was) was based on the assumption that Galen was right, and that the purpose of the dissection was to point out the truths he had laid down. The professor in charge of the dissection would read the relevant passages [from Galen's books], while a surgeon (in those days, a very lowly member of the [medical] pecking order) carried out the actual dissection, and a third member of the team, called an ostensor, would use a pointer to indicate the various organs and so on being referred to by the professor. The idea was simply to demonstrate what was already

> known, and had been known since Galen's time.[19]

When Vesalius started teaching anatomy, he dissected for his students and explained the significance of each step, rather than referring to Galen's writings. This method was so effective that it began to spread to other Italian universities and eventually to other countries. Vesalius proceeded to make important discoveries about the structure of the heart, nervous system, and muscles. In 1543, the same year that Copernicus published his masterwork arguing for the heliocentric system, Vesalius published *On the Fabric of the Human Body*. In this book, he strongly stated that physicians and medical researchers should do their own human dissections and come to their own medical conclusions without relying on ancient authors' assumptions.

Vesalius's influence remained strong well after he stopped teaching in Italy, as well as after he died in 1564. One of his students at Padua, Gabriele Fallopio (or Fallopius), started teaching anatomy in 1551 and became famous for discovering the human fallopian tubes (in the female reproductive system). Fallopio's own student, Girolamo Fabrizio, also carried on Vesalius's methods and was a professor for one of the greatest medical researchers of all time: William Harvey.

Pumping Blood

Harvey, who was born in England in 1578, got his medical degree in Padua in 1602 and later taught anatomy and surgery at London's Royal College of Physicians. In addition to his teaching duties, he did extensive research, which included repeated human dissections, through which he hoped to better understand the flow of blood through the body. At the time, nearly all doctors believed that Galen had explained the blood's movements and the heart's actions with full accuracy. According to Galen, two kinds of blood existed in the body. The first, called nutritive blood, was made in the liver and carried by the veins to the organs. The second, called vital blood, was made in the heart and carried by the arteries. Moreover, Galen claimed that the heart sucked blood out of the veins, rather than pumping blood through the body.

Harvey concluded that Galen's conception of the heart and blood, though an impressive attempt to explain these things in ancient times, was all wrong. Harvey claimed that the blood circulates through the body in a closed, circular, repeating sequence, or loop. It travels through the veins to the heart, from there to the lungs, where it picks up oxygen, and then goes back to the heart, which pumps it throughout the body via the arteries. In *On the Motion of the Heart and Blood in Animals*, he wrote,

The blood passes through the lungs and heart by the force of the ventricles, and is sent for distribution to all parts of the body, where it makes its way into the veins ... and then flows by the veins ... to the centre, from the lesser to the greater veins, and is by them finally discharged into the vena cava and right auricle [two chambers of the heart] ... it is absolutely necessary to conclude that the blood in the animal body is impelled in a circle, and is in a state of ceaseless motion.[20]

Some doctors and scientists immediately accepted Harvey's explanation of human circulation and began supporting his theories and teaching them in schools. However, a considerable number of others remained skeptical, so it took decades for his ideas to be completely accepted. Doctors struggled to accept his explanation because the means by which blood transferred from the arteries to the veins in the body's extremities was still unknown. The tiny vessels, called capillaries, that actually link the arteries and veins were too small to be seen by the naked eye. Only when microscopes powerful enough to reveal the capillaries became available was blood circulation completely understood and Harvey proven entirely correct.

By conducting human dissections, Vesalius discovered that the standard anatomy theories were all wrong.

William Harvey insisted that blood was pumped from the veins to the heart, to the lungs, and back again.

SPONTANEOUS GENERATION

When germs were first discovered during the Scientific Revolution, the consensus of scientists was that these tiny creatures played no vital role in nature. However, some did question how the creatures had come to exist. Over time, a number of European researchers came to believe that germs, like many other small living things observed in various niches of nature, suddenly appeared from nonliving matter. This theory was referred to as spontaneous generation. Part of the proof for it was that maggots were always found in decaying meat and appeared to grow spontaneously from it. What was not known at that time was that maggots were so often found in rotting meat because flies had laid eggs in the meat. It was not until the 19th and 20th centuries that scientists learned that germs reproduce like other living things and spread from one place to another via animals, people, the wind, moving water, and other natural processes.

The Early Microscopes

Revealing the existence of capillaries was only one of numerous ways the optical, or light, microscope revolutionized science and human civilization. It particularly aided the field of medicine in the 1700s and beyond. Huge amounts of modern medical research, including the groundbreaking germ theory of disease, were the direct results of the invention and steady improvement of the microscope during the Scientific Revolution.

Like the telescope, the optical microscope was not invented by a single person in a given place and time. Historians believe that both simple microscopes (having one convex lens) and compound microscopes (with two or more lenses) were created independently by several individuals. It appears that a number of unidentified European spectacle makers experimented with simple microscopes in late medieval times. These were essentially smaller versions of today's magnifying glasses. Some historians have claimed that two Dutch spectacle makers, Hans Janssen and his son, Zacharias, made a more sophisticated compound scope in 1590. However, this claim is debated, partly because it has been determined that Zacharias would have been very young in 1590.

What is known for sure is that Galileo built a crude compound microscope in 1609. Dutch astronomer Christiaan Huygens then made a

Shown here is a reproduction of an early microscope.

Antonie van Leeuwenhoek used a microscope similar to this to discover germs.

two-lens scope a few decades later. It was Galileo's friend, German botanist Giovanni Faber, who in 1625, coined the term "microscope." He borrowed from Greek to name the invention, combining the words for "small" and "to look at." Most of the earliest microscopes, especially the simple ones having a single lens, were considered novelties. Scientists did not recognize their potential in research. The man who brought these scopes to the attention of biologists and other scientists, and thereby came to be called the father of microscopy, was Antonie van Leeuwenhoek. Born in Holland in 1632, he owned and ran a clothes store in the town of Delft.

Leeuwenhoek's passionate hobby—grinding glass into fine, polished lenses and using them as magnifying glasses—eventually made him famous. The series of single-lens scopes he made over the course of nearly five decades were of very high quality. The best of them magnified images of objects 300 times. That made them more powerful than even the best compound scopes of his era. The reason that Leeuwenhoek's lenses were so effective, modern experts speculate, may have been that his grinding and polishing process was far superior to the ones employed by other researchers. Leeuwenhoek closely guarded the secret of the process, which remains a mystery to this day.

The initial objects Leeuwenhoek observed through his instruments were common ones, such as insects, leaves, salt crystals, pepper grains, and his own hairs and bodily fluids. A careful researcher, he took exhaustive notes describing the magnified images. He also asked acquaintances—who were better artists than he was—to look through the lenses and draw detailed pictures of what they saw.

Germs

In the 1670s, Leeuwenhoek made what was to be his greatest discovery. Seemingly swimming in pond water and other liquids he studied were tiny creatures that were invisible to the unaided eye. He called them "animalcules." As time went on, he found them in practically every material he viewed in his scopes, including food, human and animal wastes, the bodies of insects, and scrapings from people's teeth (including his own). Leeuwenhoek penned one of his descriptions of the creatures, which would eventually be named "germs," after examining some pond water in 1674:

The motion of most of the animalcules in the water was so swift and so various, upward, downwards, and round about, that 'twas wonderful to see. And I judge that some of

OBSERVING WITH A MICROSCOPE

This excerpt from Robert Hooke's *Micrographia* describes his microscopic observation of tiny pores in burnt vegetable matter:

Charcoal, or a Vegetable burnt black, affords an object no less pleasant than instructive, for if you take a small round Charcoal, and break it short with your fingers, you may perceive it to break with a very smooth and sleek surface, almost like the surface of black sealing Wax; this surface, if it be look'd on with an ordinary Microcscope, does manifest abundance of those pores which are also visible to the eye in many kinds of Wood ... If a better Microscope be made use of, there will appear an infinite company of exceedingly small, and very regular pores, so thick and so orderly set, and so close to one another, that they leave very little room or space between them to be fill'd with a solid body.[1]

1. Robert Hooke, *Micrographia*. New Delhi, India: Prabhat Prakashan, 1998. PDF e-book.

these little creatures were above a thousand times smaller than the smallest ones I have ever yet seen upon the rind of cheese in wheat flour, mold, and the like.[21]

In 1683, after observing a host of germs in some scrapings taken from his own teeth, Leeuwenhoek claimed, "All the people living in our United Netherlands are not as many as the living animals that I carry in my own mouth this very day."[22] He recognized that knowledge of these tiny creatures might be important to science and wanted to share observations with the Royal Society. From 1674 until his death in 1723, Leeuwenhoek sent many letters to that London-based organization. In one of the first, he modestly said, "I beg you and the Gentlemen under whose eyes this happens to come to bear in mind that my observations and opinions are only the result of my own impulse and curiosity."[23]

At first, the scientists at the Royal Society were fascinated by Leeuwenhoek's claims about seeing minuscule animals in water and other substances, but they became disappointed and even somewhat suspicious when they could not replicate his experiments. During the later years of the Scientific Revolution, the Royal Society set a new standard: Its members demanded that any new scientific discovery must be verified by having other scientists repeat the experiment performed by the discoverer. If it could not be repeated, it was likely not valid. This remains true of science today. English naturalist Robert Hooke was the society's curator of experiments. Over and over again, he kept trying to reproduce Leeuwenhoek's conditions and technique using a scope of similar design and size. In November 1677, Hooke was finally successful and managed to see the germs for himself. This discovery was later shared with other members of the Royal Society:

> *Mr. Hooke had all the week discovered great numbers of exceedingly small animals swimming to and fro. They appeared of the bigness of a mite through a glass, that magnified about an hundred thousand times in build; and consequently it was judged, that they were near an hundred thousand times less than a mite ... They were observed to have all manner of motions to and fro in the water; and by all, who saw them, they were [truly] believed to be animals. They were seen by Mr. Henshaw, Sir Christopher Wren, Sir John Hoskyns, Sir Jonas Moore, Dr. Mapletoft, Mr. Hill, Dr. Croune, Dr. Grew, Mr. Aubrey, and [many] others; so that*

> *there was no longer any doubt of Mr. Leewenhoeck's discovery.*[24]

At the time, no one, including Hooke, his colleagues, and Leeuwenhoek himself, had any idea what the microscopic creatures were or how they had come into existence. It appeared to them that they were perfectly harmless, so they did not think to connect them to disease. In fact, the consensus of scientists was that the tiny animals served no specific purpose in nature—an assumption that would be found to be completely wrong about two centuries later.

Micrographia

The optical microscope remained a valuable tool to scientists, both amateur and professional, during the final century of the Scientific Revolution. Leeuwenhoek continued to study all manner of objects, as did hundreds of other amateurs in both Europe and the American colonies. Robert Hooke constructed his own microscopes, with which he performed hundreds of experiments. His book *Micrographia* was intended to demonstrate to scientists and the public alike the potential use of the instrument in biology. It contained detailed drawings, done by Hooke himself, of many of the magnified images he had produced. Among the drawings were a fly's compound eye, plant cells, and the bodies of lice, fleas, and other insects.

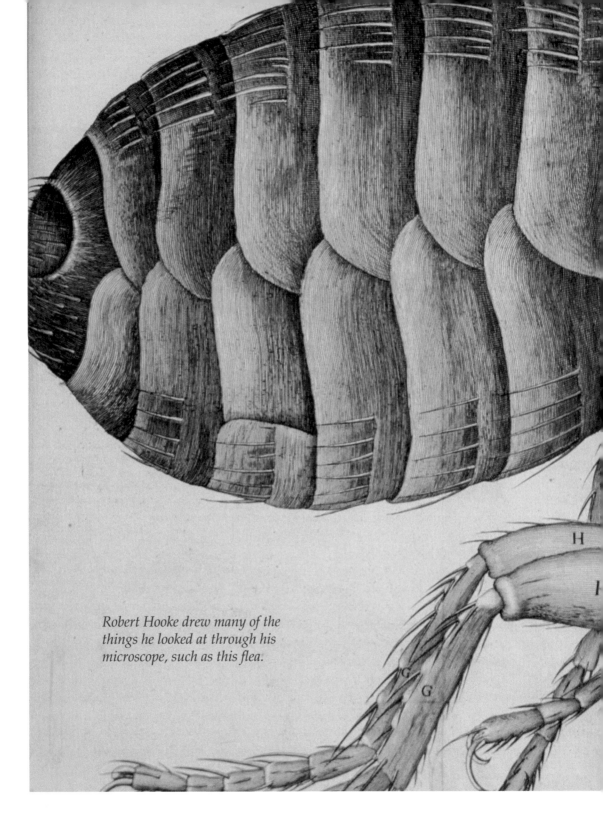

Robert Hooke drew many of the things he looked at through his microscope, such as this flea.

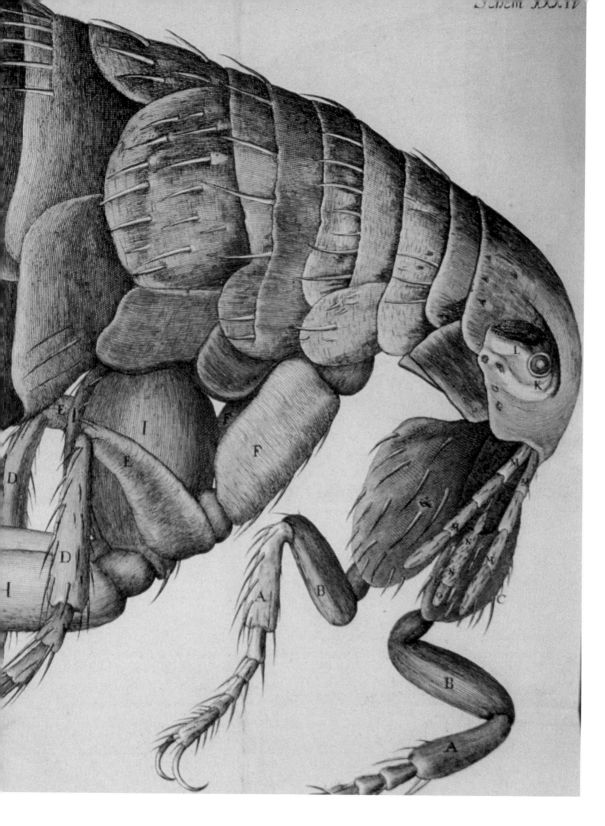

Hooke's book and others like it became widely popular, in large part because of such drawings. According to scholar Lisa Jardine: "The tiny living organisms depicted in seventeenth-century scientific engravings appeared arrestingly strange and beautiful. When [one noted researcher] first looked at an insect through a lens, his immediate thought was to seek out the best contemporary artists to record the exquisite beauty of what he saw."[25] These artistic renderings also inspired numerous individuals to become biologists and other scientists, another crucial contribution made by the microscope within the Scientific Revolution.

CHAPTER SIX

SIR ISAAC NEWTON

The Scientific Revolution helped establish a new era in astronomy, beginning with Copernicus's heliocentric theory. Humans were slowly, more accurately mapping out the solar system. Another question that could now be posed, however, was what caused the movement of the stars and planets? The ancient Greeks certainly did not know what kept celestial bodies in orbit and could only offer guesses. Johannes Kepler, who discovered that planets move in ellipses around the sun, thought maybe the planetary orbits occurred through magnetic forces. René Descartes theorized that all the space between planets and stars was made up of an invisible material that held everything in place with pressure.

In the last century of the Scientific Revolution, English scientist Robert Boyle laid all other theories to rest concerning how Earth was suspended in space while orbiting the sun. He determined that outer space was a vacuum, meaning it contained nothing at all. Isaac Newton then contributed his theory that there was indeed a force that kept Earth in orbit—but it was gravity, not magnetism. Newton's theory was called universal gravitation, and he established a set of laws of motion that could be applied to both objects on Earth and in space. This discovery made Newton commonly regarded as the greatest scientist of the Scientific Revolution. Today, his work continues to shape generations of scientists and mathematicians, and he is regarded as one of the most intelligent humans to ever live.

Perfectly Balanced

Newton's proposal meant that objects move the same way in the far reaches of the universe as they do on Earth. This was an enormous revelation. Before his time, most researchers assumed that whatever forces made earthly objects

Isaac Newton changed the fields of science and mathematics forever.

BOYLE'S SILENT VOID

The idea that a vacuum, or empty void, could not exist in nature was advocated by numerous ancient thinkers, as well as many early modern scientists. They believed that outer space was filled with an invisible material that many called the ether. Robert Boyle, however, proved that a vacuum could exist by pumping the air out of a glass container. In the years that followed, several other scientists suggested that a large-scale vacuum might exist in outer space. If so, it was a silent void, as one of Boyle's experiments showed that sound cannot travel in a vacuum. Sound moves in waves, and those waves need a physical medium (such as the air on Earth) to travel. In a vacuum, sound waves simply have no way of traveling.

move and kept those objects firmly on Earth's surface were different and separate from the forces that made Earth move around the sun. Newton's first major feat was to show that the same force was at work on Earth and in the heavens. Therefore, that force—gravity—must be universal.

Newton claimed that his first concepts of gravity came when he saw an apple fall from a tree. Like other scientists, he realized that the apple fell because some mysterious force pulled it and other earthly objects toward the planet's center. The question that started forming in his mind was: How far would that force continue to work? If he stood on the highest mountain on Earth and dropped an object, would it fall and hit the ground in the same way the apple fell from the tree? If so, that indicated that the

force was strong enough to work over extreme earthly distances. It seemed only logical to him, therefore, that it would do the same over the massive distances in space as well. Newton theorized that the moon might be bound to Earth by the same force that worked on the apple. If so, the moon is "falling" toward Earth and does not plunge right onto Earth, causing huge destruction, because the smaller body possesses a considerable forward motion. In the words of science historian Gale E. Christianson,

Envisioning the moon as a giant apple, Newton developed the idea of how gravity works. The satellite's tendency to move away from Earth in a straight line is counteracted by the inward pull of gravity, which produces an orbit, much as an object on

EINSTEIN BACKS NEWTON UP

In the early 20th century, German scientist Albert Einstein offered an alternative description of how gravity works. He argued that gravity is not a property of objects but a property of space itself. Einstein said that space is made of an invisible fabric with an elastic, or bendable, quality. Planets and other objects interact with this hidden fabric by sinking into it. Objects with little mass sink only a tiny bit, he said, while more massive objects create deeper depressions in the fabric. Earth appears to attract the moon because the smaller body rolls "downhill" into the depression created by the larger one. This corresponds to Earth pulling on the moon, in Newtonian terms. Modern scientists point out that Newton's formula for gravity works the same way and remains perfectly valid in Einstein's version of space.

Albert Einstein's explanation of how space works is in agreement with Newton's.

a string when it is whirled around one's head. The moon is perfectly balanced between the tendency to move outward ... and the inward pull of Earth.[26]

In the same way, Newton determined, the sun's gravity attracts Earth and the other planets. These bodies are inclined to fall toward the sun as a result, but their forward motion cancels out gravity's pull and keeps them in orbit around the larger star. Furthermore, Newton concluded, gravity must work in the very same manner throughout the known universe. To demonstrate this, he developed a mathematical formula that described the balance. Using his equation, he identified a gravitational constant (a number that represents the force of gravity and can be applied to everything), typically represented as G, and that constant is still used today.

Newton showed that, using this equation, anyone could quite easily calculate the amount of attraction exerted by one object on another. One could also determine the masses of the objects in the solar system. Knowing the distance between Earth and the moon, scientists used Newton's formula to discover the masses of these bodies. Once these figures were known, they could calculate the sun's mass and from there, the masses of other planets. Mercury, the closest planet to the sun, was found to be 20 times smaller than Earth. Jupiter,

the largest planet, turned out to be 318 times more massive than Earth. The theory of universal gravitation revolutionized science. Newton's scientific principles convinced other scientists that the same laws they were discovering about Earth could also be applied to outer space.

Universal Uses

Researchers found that Newton's formula for universal gravitation could be used to mathematically verify Kepler's laws of planetary motion. Kepler had created those laws by investigating Tycho Brahe's detailed observations of the planets' yearly motions. In contrast, Newton's formula created the same laws indirectly—through mathematics. Two different paths had been used to reach the same astronomical destination. Scientists also found that they could use Newton's formula to find out the strength of gravity's pull on Earth's surface and the surfaces of other worlds. A person's weight on one of those worlds could then be calculated. The more massive the planet, the larger its gravity will be, and vice versa. An individual would then expect to weigh less on a planet smaller than Earth and weigh more on a planet bigger than Earth.

Still another implication of universal gravitation derived from Newton's formula is the phenomenon known as escape velocity. This concept is important to rocket science, as it is the speed at which an object needs to move in order to escape the gravity of another object. Earth's escape velocity is roughly 7 miles (11.2 km) per second. A rocket must attain that speed to break free of the gravitational attraction exerted by the planet. In comparison, imagine trying to launch a rocket from the surface of the planet Neptune (if it had a solid surface). Neptune is bigger than Earth, so the rocket would need to attain a higher escape velocity to break free of Neptune's gravitational pull. The highest escape velocity in the solar system is that of the sun—about 385 miles (619.6 km) per second. By contrast, Earth's moon has an escape velocity of only 1.5 miles (2.4 km) per second. That means that the astronauts who visited the moon had a much easier time getting off the moon than they had leaving Earth.

Newton's Three Laws of Motion

Newton pointed out that all the objects moving through space must be governed by universal laws. He determined three such basic laws, which he published along with his ideas about gravity in his 1687 work *Philosophiæ Naturalis Principia Mathematica*. (This title translates to *Mathematical Principles of Natural Philosophy* in English, but it is commonly referred to as the *Principia*.) These laws were among his most valuable contributions to science and mathematics.

The first of the three laws of motion deals with the phenomenon of inertia, which is the tendency of objects to resist change. In order for an object to move, Newton wrote, some kind of outside force must push or pull on it, because if that did not happen, the object would remain motionless, or at rest. His law of inertia states that such an object will either stay at rest or move in a straight line at a steady rate of speed unless acted on by an outside force. Astronauts, for example, appear to be floating around in space; that is because they are not being acted on by Earth's gravity. If an astronaut threw a ball while doing a spacewalk, that ball could theoretically travel infinitely. It would only stop if a gravitational field, such as that from the sun, took hold of it during its flight.

Newton's second law of motion deals with the nature and size of the forces that might act to make an object move. Essentially, it says that such a force will do one or more of three things to an object: speed it up, or accelerate it; slow it down, or decelerate it; or alter the direction in which the object is moving. Much of what happens depends on the object's mass: The greater the mass, the stronger the force needed to accelerate it, decelerate it, or change its direction of motion. A good example of the second law is when someone fires a cannon. One force, the gunpowder explosion in the rear of the cannon, causes the stationary cannonball to accelerate. If someone fired the cannon in outer space, in a region far away from planets and

PHILOSOPHIÆ

NATURALIS

PRINCIPIA

MATHEMATICA.

Autore *JS. NEWTON*, *Trin. Coll. Cantab. Soc.* Matheseos Professore *Lucasiano,* & Societatis Regalis Sodali.

IMPRIMATUR·

S. PEPYS, *Reg. Soc.* PRÆSES.

Julii 5. 1686.

LONDINI,

Jussu *Societatis Regiæ* ac Typis *Josephi Streater.* Prostant Venales apud *Sam. Smith* ad insignia Principis *Walliæ* in Cœmiterio D. *Pauli,* aliosq; nonnullos Bibliopolas. *Anno* MDCLXXXVII.

Newton's most famous book (shown here) described his three laws of motion.

other bodies exerting gravity, the ball would, as stated in the first law, keep on moving along in a straight line. If the cannon were fired on Earth, however, a second force, gravity, soon acts on the moving ball in two ways. First, gravity causes it to decelerate, and second, gravity makes the ball move downward in a curved arc toward the ground. The ball's mass also matters. If it weighs 20 pounds (9 kg), the explosion will propel it a certain distance before gravity pulls it to the ground. On the other hand, if the ball weighs 50 pounds (22.6 kg), the same explosion will propel it a considerably shorter distance before gravity decelerates it and pulls it downward.

Newton's third law of motion deals with an important consequence of an object's motion. It states that for every action, there is an equal and opposite reaction. One way of looking at this situation is that forces occur in pairs. A person walking on Earth's surface, for example, is exerting a force on the ground with every step. At the same time their foot pushes downward, the ground is pushing back with an equal force, which balances the steps out. Without this equal and opposite force, simply taking a walk could send a person flying off into space or down into the planet's core. Another familiar example of Newton's third law in action is firing off a rocket. The force of the hot gases shooting backward from the rocket's lower end causes an equal amount of force in the opposite direction. This takes the form of the rocket's powerful forward motion.

Father of the Scientific Revolution

Newton's book *Principia* was one of the greatest achievements of the Scientific Revolution. Copernicus, Brahe, Francis Bacon, Kepler, Galileo, and others had laid a firm foundation for him. Newton always insisted that he was only able to accomplish his amazing breakthroughs because of the hard work of past scientific heroes. Despite his modesty, however, Newton thought decades beyond his predecessors, and in doing so, he opened the way for the emergence of modern science.

In the centuries following Newton's death in 1727, science—especially the disciplines of physics, astronomy, mathematics, chemistry, and optics—has changed human society in ways too numerous to list. Among Newton's major accomplishments, he finalized the scientific method initially developed by Ibn al-Haytham, Galileo, the Bacons, and Descartes by showing how it could be consistently applied to complex theories in a wide range of scientific disciplines. Newton also revealed how the universe works, showing that a small set of basic mathematical laws can explain the motions of almost all the bodies in nature. That made it possible for later astronomers to form theories about the origins and structure of the cosmos, which

Isaac Newton is buried in this tomb in Westminster Abbey.

reached their height of success in the mid-to-late 20th century.

Newton made it easier for astronomers, physicists, and other scientists to formulate and prove fresh theories by inventing a new form of mathematics: calculus. He developed calculus with German mathematician Gottfried Leibniz. Newton's equations and laws concerning gravity and motion made powered flight—which finally took off in the 20th century—possible. That quickly led to airplanes, rockets, and space travel. It is no wonder that Newton's name has become synonymous with the Scientific Revolution and the development of modern science.

THE RIPPLE EFFECT OF THE SCIENTIFIC REVOLUTION

The Scientific Revolution laid the groundwork for what is known today as modern science. It challenged and transformed major ideas that had been taken for granted for centuries. It also went on to change the world in a variety of other ways, including inspiring the European Enlightenment. The Enlightenment was an intellectual movement in the 18th century that spread all over Europe and the American colonies. The Enlightenment took place because of how the Scientific Revolution encouraged the smartest minds to challenge tradition—especially when it came to religious authority.

Copernicus, Galileo, and Newton challenged conventions and proved that there was so much more for humans to learn about the natural world around them. Scientific advancement did not end with the ancient Greeks. The Enlightenment took this example and applied it to society in general, instead of specifically to science. The thinkers who contributed to the Enlightenment aimed to make society better. They applied the rational, logic-driven practices of the Scientific Revolution to economic and social issues, and the result was a new confidence in humankind's ability to improve and innovate.

A New Age

Those who led the Enlightenment encouraged society to become more open-minded, progressive, and thoughtful. There was a heavy influence on education in order to separate the new age of logic and reason from the old, superstitious traditions. The major concepts of the Enlightenment included recognizing that nature works through scientific principles, that the unknown should not be feared, that all religions should be respected, and that human understanding comes from experience.

The most important result of the intellectual growth achieved by the Enlightenment was the concept that humans have basic rights, and these need to be respected by everyone—including governments and churches. English, French, and American colonial legislators all began to think that laws could be made more fair and just. Individuals began promoting the ideas of freedom of thought, self-expression, public assembly, and freedom to choose government leaders. These fundamental concepts inspired the colonies to break away from England and establish a new country: the United States of America. The Founding Fathers were particularly influenced by the Enlightenment and Englishman John Locke, who argued that monarchs were bad for basic human rights. In his essay *Two Treatises of Government*, Locke wrote that monarchs should not have complete control and they should be held accountable for their actions by the people they rule. Locke believed that a government should be constructed based on the needs and will of the people that it is governing and that the most important

responsibility of that government is to protect the civil rights of those people.

With John Locke and the Enlightenment as a foundation, the first modern democracy was created in North America. The ideas of liberty and equality spread across the world and influenced dozens of other countries and their governments. This was the revolutionary result of the advancements made in the Scientific Revolution. The Scientific Revolution proved that the human mind is limitless and that nature's mysteries can be studied and understood. It signified that if humans can understand their environment better, they can understand themselves better, and there is no limit to their growth and knowledge.

The Scientific Revolution taught the human race that there is a lot of knowledge to be gained and that no one will ever know it all. Today, medical and astronomical advancements continue. New cures and treatments for diseases are being uncovered and tested every day, leading to longer, healthier lives. New planets that might sustain life outside of the solar system continue to be discovered. Astronauts continue to travel further out in space to learn more about an environment of which there is still little knowledge. Earth itself is seeing the effects of decades of technological advancement and human invention. Humankind has only recently understood the planet and is now faced with the dilemma of how to sustain it. However, there is hope for future generations of Copernicuses, Galileos, and Newtons to continue the revolution that was sparked centuries ago.

Introduction:
A New Science
1. Lisa Jardine, *Ingenious Pursuits: Building the Scientific Revolution*. New York, NY: Anchor Books, 2000, p. 363.

Chapter One:
Grandfathers of Science
2. Quoted in W. K. C. Guthrie, *The Greek Philosophers: From Thales to Aristotle*. Abingdon, UK: Routledge, 2012, p. 32.

3. Quoted in Benjamin Wiker, *The Catholic Church & Science: Answering the Questions, Exposing the Myths*. Charlotte, NC: TAN Books, 2011, PDF e-book.

4. Quoted in Adrian Johnstone, "Galileo and the Pendulum Clock," Adrian Johnstone's Homepage, July 8, 2009, accessed December 1, 2017. www.cs.rhul.ac.uk/~adrian/timekeeping/galileo.

5. Steven Shapin, *The Scientific Revolution*. Chicago, IL: University of Chicago Press, 1996, pp. 75–76.

Chapter Two:
The Copernican Revolution
6. Nicolaus Copernicus, *On the Revolutions of the Heavenly Spheres*, Charles Glenn Wallis, trans. Amherst, NY: Prometheus Books, 1995, p. 17.

7. Copernicus, *On the Revolutions*, p. 17.

8. Thomas S. Kuhn, *The Copernican Revolution: Planetary Astronomy in the Development of Western Thought*. New York, NY: MJF, 1985, p. 144.

9. Giordano Bruno, "The Ash Wednesday Supper," Stanley L. Jaki, trans. math.dartmouth.edu/~matc/Readers/renaissance.astro/6.1. Supper.html. HTML e-book.

Chapter Three:
Far-Seeing

10. Steven Shapin, *A Social History of Truth: Civility and Science in Seventeenth-Century England*. Chicago, IL: University of Chicago Press, 1994, p. 194.

11. Quoted in John Robert Christianson, *On Tycho's Island: Tycho Brahe, Science, and Culture in the Sixteenth Century*. New York, NY: Cambridge University Press, 2002, p. 22.

12. James MacLachlan, *Galileo Galilei: First Physicist*. New York, NY: Oxford University Press, 1999, p. 50.

13. Quoted in Edward Harrison, *Masks of the Universe: Changing Ideas on the Nature of the Cosmos*. Cambridge, UK: Cambridge University Press, 2003, p. 94.

Chapter Four:
The Scientific Method

14. H. D. P. Lee, "Introduction" in Aristotle, *Meteorology*. Cambridge, MA: Harvard University Press, 2015, p. xxvi.

15. Jim Al-Khalili, "The First True Scientist," BBC News, January 4, 2009. news.bbc.co.uk/2/hi/science/nature/7810846.stm.

16. Martyn Shuttleworth, "History of the Scientific Method," Explorable.com, August 18, 2009. explorable.com/history-of-the-scientific-method.

17. Roger Bacon, *On Experimental Science*, Internet Medieval Source Book, accessed December 5, 2017. sourcebooks.fordham.edu/source/bacon2.asp.

18. Quoted in Raymond Séroul, *Programming for Mathematicians*, Donal O'Shea, trans. New York, NY: Springer, 2012, p. 4.

Chapter Five:
Blood, Germs, and the Microscope

19. John Gribbin, *The Fellowship: The Story of a Revolution*. London, UK: Penguin, 2006, PDF e-book.

20. William Harvey, *On the Motion of the Heart and Blood in Animals*. London, UK: George Bell and Sons, 1889, p. 71.

21. Quoted in Edward Dolnick, *The Seeds of Life: From Aristotle to da Vinci, from Sharks' Teeth to Frogs' Pants, the Long and Strange Quest to Discover Where Babies Come From*. New York, NY: Basic Books, 2017, PDF e-book.

22. Quoted in Charles-Edward Amory Winslow, *The Conquest of Epidemic Disease: A Chapter in the History of Ideas*. Madison, WI: University of Wisconsin Press, 1980, p. 158.

23. Quoted in Jardine, *Ingenious Pursuits*, p. 89.

24. Thomas Birch, *The History of the Royal Society in London*, vol. 3. London, UK: A. Millar in the Strand, 1757, p. 352.

25. Jardine, *Ingenious Pursuits*, pp. 101–102.

Chapter Six:
Sir Isaac Newton

26. Gale E. Christianson, *Isaac Newton*. New York, NY: Oxford University Press, 2005, p. 29.

Books

Gribbin, John. *The Scientists: A History of Science Told Through the Lives of Its Greatest Inventors*. New York, NY: Random House, 2002.
  This book recounts scientific advancement in history, focusing on the scientists themselves, starting with Nicolaus Copernicus.

Kuhn, Thomas. *The Structure of Scientific Revolutions: 50th Anniversary*. Chicago, IL: University of Chicago Press, 2012.
  Kuhn outlines scientific progress by illustrating that ideas come from breakthrough moments outside of normal science.

Losure, Mary. *Isaac the Alchemist: Secrets of Isaac Newton, Reveal'd*. Somerville, MA: Candlewick, 2017.
  Losure focuses on Isaac Newton's childhood and how he became one of the greatest minds in history.

Pagden, Anthony. *The Enlightenment: And Why It Still Matters*. Oxford, UK: Oxford University Press, 2013.
  This book is a historical account of the Enlightenment, the period of thought and advancement that came directly after the Scientific Revolution.

Principe, Lawrence. *Scientific Revolution: A Very Short Introduction*. Oxford, UK: Oxford University Press, 2011.
  This book explores the discoveries made during the Scientific Revolution, told from the perspectives of the historical characters themselves, such as Nicolaus Copernicus, Galileo Galilei, and Isaac Newton.

Websites

Eric Weisstein's World of Biography
scienceworld.wolfram.com/biography/letters
    This website contains a collection of scientific biographies.

The Galileo Project
galileo.rice.edu
    This website is a source of information on the life and work of Galileo, one of the most famous scientists of the Scientific Revolution.

Guided History: Sir Isaac Newton and the Scientific Revolution
blogs.bu.edu/guidedhistory/moderneurope/antonio-rebello
    This website is a guide to the Scientific Revolution through primary and secondary sources about Newton's life.

The Medieval Sourcebook
sourcebooks.fordham.edu/halsall/mod/modsbook09.asp
    This website, hosted by Fordham University, contains a list of primary sources from the Scientific Revolution.

Nicolaus Copernicus
starchild.gsfc.nasa.gov/docs/StarChild/whos_who_level2/copernicus.html
    This website, sponsored by NASA, contains a biography of one of the fathers of the Scientific Revolution, as well as links to other pages about astronomy.

Picture Credits

Cover photo 12/Contributor/Universal Images Group/Getty Images; pp. 6–7 (background) Stefano Bianchetti/Contributor/Corbis Historical/Getty Images; p. 6 (left and right) Leemage/Universal Images Group/Getty Images; p. 6 (middle) Stock Montage/Contributor/Archive Photos/Getty Images; p. 7 (left) Courtesy of RIJSK Museum; p. 7 (right) Claritas/Wikimedia Commons; p. 11 Print Collector/Contributor/Hulton Fine Art Collection/Getty Images; pp. 14–15 National Museum in Cracow, Poland/Bridgeman Images; p. 17 Hulton Archive/Stringer/Hulton Archive/Getty Images; p. 18 Bianchetti/Leemage/Bridgeman Images; p. 20 Mondadori Portfolio/Contributor/Hulton Fine Art Collection/Getty Images; p. 22 Panos Karas/Shutterstock.com; pp. 26, 89 Science & Society Picture Library/Contributor/SSPL/Getty Images; p. 29 SCIENCE SOURCE/Science Source/Getty Images; p. 31 DEA/G. DAGLI ORTI/Contributor/De Agostini/Getty Images; pp. 32–33 Photo Josse/Leemage/Contributor/Corbis Historical/Getty Images; pp. 34–35 Gimas/Shutterstock.com; pp. 37, 67 UniversalImagesGroup/Universal Images Group/Getty Images; pp. 40, 42–43 Print Collector/Contributor/Hulton Archive/Getty Images; pp. 46–47 Bettmann/Contributor/Bettmann/Getty Images; p. 49 NASA/JPL/DLR; pp. 52, 60 Photos.com/PHOTOS.com>>/Thinkstock; p. 58 Universal Images Group/Universal Images Group Editorial/Getty Images; p. 62 Private Collection/Bridgeman Images; p. 64 Imagno/Contributor/Hulton Fine Art Collection/Getty Images; pp. 70–71, 86 Courtesy of the Library of Congress; pp. 72–73 Wellcome Collection/Wellcome Collection; pp. 75, 76 Science Museum, London/Wellcome Collection; pp. 80–81 Courtesy of U.S. National Library of Medicine; p. 84 Georgios Kollidas/Shutterstock.com; p. 91 PA Images/Alamy Stock Photo.

About the Author

Caroline Kennon is a college librarian originally from Yonkers, New York. She got her bachelor's and master's degrees in English from St. Bonaventure University in Western New York and her master's in library science from the University at Buffalo. She is an avid reader, a novice cyclist, and a cheese addict. She currently lives in South Buffalo, New York—the winters really aren't that bad.